FOR SHE IS THE TREE OF LIFE

EDITED BY

VALERIE KACK-BRICE

MJF BOOKS

NEW YORK

Published by MJF Books
Fine Communications
Two Lincoln Square
60 West 66th Street
New York, NY 10023

Library of Congress Catalog Card Number 96-78821
ISBN 1-56731-193-8

Manufactured in the United States of America on acid-free paper

MJF Books and the MJF colophon are trademarks of Fine Creative Media, Inc.

10   9   8   7   6   5   4   3   2   1

MY LIPS MOVE

My grandmother opens her mouth
and her mother wakes.
We are wrapped in one
rainbow shawl.
Somewhere hidden,
their words whisper as snow
held in the sky.
Their bones that once shaped
their bodies lift an arm.
Our hands move.
All the ancestor's arms write
with my pen.

Mary Freericks

IN MEMORY OF MY DEAR GRANDMOTHERS

Carrie Adella Jones

and

Mary Nina Kack

Gratitude has inspired this collection of writings, and so it is also with boundless gratitude that I acknowledge the following:

My husband for his endless support.

My son for his joyfulness and light.

Ann Jealous for her enthusiasm when I tell her my ideas
and for her useful editing comments, but mostly
for her loyalty, loving support, and belief in me.

D. Hanson, my writing partner and friend, for her daily listening,
generous heart, and unquestionable succor.

Ronnie Paul, Jeff Kane, Karla Arens, Michael Fox, Susan Solinsky,
Liz Collins, Jeff Hattem, D Hanson, and Sandra Rockman,
members of my writing group, for reading the massive first draft and
most especially for their consistent intellectual nourishment.

Jane Hotchkiss for her astute editorial criticism.

Iris Deznan for her resourcefulness, belief in my writing, and humor.

Carol Cooper for her excellent library search skills.

Judith Ritter Leigh for her middle-of-the-night
"messing with" the manuscript.

Mary Jane Ryan at Conari Press for her insight and willingness to
take on this project and for her direction and guidance.

My parents who gave me a chance to know my grandmothers.

My sisters, for loving my grandmothers as much as I do.

CONTENTS

A Word to the Wise, 115

A Stitch in Time, 151

Bone of My Bones: A Grandmother Workbook, 199

INTRODUCTION

From Albuquerque, I took Highway 40 west to Acoma pueblo. The sky was a poem of rain clouds and blue, ghostly white shimmering veils, and black, ominous streaks, low to the ground. My grandmother had died a few months before; I wasn't yet conscious that this journey was about her and the gifts I would glean from her passing.

On the mesa, late winter, the early spring population was low. Only three families live there year round. Accustomed to visitors passing through their village streets, these mesa dwellers are hopeful to make a sale from their hand-built black-on-white pottery. The eye travels around corners, through doorways, to the smallest detail—a pottery shard glistening in sunlight—and beyond adobe structures and lone cottonwood, to cornfields carpeting the distance between this and the next mesa.

Descending from the mesa top I placed my hand in notched handholds on the sandstone walls to steady myself on the narrow steps, and my head spun with images of rock and graffiti and water-washed crevices. My hand in those little perfect places . . . touching where people have touched since that first ascent. I felt a jolt, like an electrical impulse, plugged into the vibrations of those hearty, determined ancestors.

I cried all the way back to Albuquerque, thinking about my grandmother. Without her, I feel cut loose, like a balloon caught by the wind, seeking its ballast. Those people on the mesa know details of individual lives, family milestones, and community events for hundreds, perhaps thousands, of years. They are tied not only to each other by blood and by a determination to protect and contain their culture, but also to their homes, passed from generation to generation through the youngest female child, and to the land—with its history and its timelessness. These people know who they are. Named and naming, belonging.

I returned home with the seed of an idea that would winter over, like the bulbs I planted in my grandmother's memory. I would hold on to her, catch the cord, by harnessing the story of her life, and create a context for making meaning of my own history.

As a psychotherapist I have seen many women who have struggled to heal their loss of childhood. I began to see, as in my own life, a thread of powerful memories involving grandmothers woven throughout their lives. Some women are grateful for the modeling and support their grandmothers gave. As children, many were desperate for the connection to a loving presence, relieved to have structure and routine from a mature caregiver. For many, snapping peas and kneading dough were simple activities that slowed the pace of life and marked significantly the passage of time shared between granddaughter and grandmother. In these moments grandmothers transmitted history, wisdom, practical information, and concern to granddaughters. For many women, their grandmother's care served as a balm for mistreatment and loneliness; grandmother became healer to a wounded spirit.

For other women, grandmother is a frightening presence. She is abrupt or overbearing, distant or cool. And sometimes her criticism motivates decisions toward a particular profession, lifestyle or behavior. Again, even in the disappointment of an unsupportive grandmother, women gain potent lessons about loving. Either in the joy of her caring or the sorrow of her criticism, women find healing. *Grandmother* is rarely a neutral moniker.

For some women, what is most memorable about their grandmothers is a lifestyle, skill, or particular quality. Some grandmothers have great humor, others a kind of stoicism that makes them strong in the face of hardship. Their modeling offers many kinds of gifts or lessons. These remembrances can become muted or distorted with time. Time distorts memory. Perhaps we just forget. But also, we may need to see "grandmother" in a particular way; as women exploring our own identities, many of us seek a model for a feminine hero.

Observation tells me there is a unique quality of relationship between grandparent and grandchild that is different from the parent/child relationship. Perhaps grandchildren have enough distance from the older generation to see the factors that influenced their parents' lives; from this vantage point they can come to an understanding of a parent's failings and, eventually, to forgiveness. Finally, through appreciation of our elders and what they gave or couldn't give, we come to know ourselves.

Motivation for this anthology came from knowing my grandmother. I wanted to keep her essence alive, for me and for my children's children. Like many others, I am hungry for a connection to the past. I wanted to take with me a sense of another time, a slower pace and a closer relationship to the activities that fill basic needs. I wanted to remember her gifts to me. And I wanted to feel community with other women writing about their grandmothers.

The writers who contributed are between sixteen and eighty-five years old; some have grandchildren themselves. Their grandmothers, both real and imaginary, lived during this and the past century, and represent a diversity of cultural, racial, and class histories. These writers have thought about this relationship and felt compelled to express its meaning. Their writing reveals a need to keep alive this unique connection.

This anthology is a way for us to share our expressions of gratitude for our grandmothers and will perhaps encourage the reader to examine her own grandmother stories and legacy.

"The very commonplaces of life
are components of its eternal mystery."
Gertrude Atherton

THE CUT
OF HER CLOTH

While many of our grandmothers led simple lives, some lived simply in the middle of extraordinary circumstances, demonstrating great courage, fortitude and commitment. Undaunted by specific events, they were tenacious in their survival, hope, and connection to family. For some grand-daughters, the example of how their grandmothers lived offered valuable lessons and gave gifts, sometimes even resulting in a determination to live differently. For others, a particular quality of being, such as eccentricity, stoicism, or dignity, is most notable.

FOR SHE IS A TREE OF LIFE

Marge Piercy

In the cramped living room of my childhood
between sagging rough-skinned sofa that made me itch
and swaybacked chair surrounded by ashtrays
where my father read every word of the paper
shrouded in blue smoke, coughed rusty phlegm
and muttering doom, the rug was a factory
oriental and the pattern called tree of life.

My mother explained as we plucked a chicken
tree of life: I was enthralled and Hannah
my grandmother hummed for me the phrase
from liturgy: Eytz khayim hee l'makhazikim
bo v'kol nitee-voteh-ho shalom:
for she is a tree of life to all who hold her fast,
and the fruit of her branches is peace.

I see her big bosomed and tall as a maple
and in her veins the beige sugar of desire
running sometimes hard, surging skyward
and sometimes sunk down into the roots
and clay and the bones of rabbits and foxes
lying in the same bed at last becoming one.

I see her opening into flushed white
blossoms the bees crawl into. I see her
branches dipping under the weight of the yield,
the crimson, the yellow and russet globes,
apples fallen beneath the deer crunch.
Yellow jackets in the cobalt afternoon buzz
drunken from cracked fruit oozing juice.

We all fit through her branches or creep
through her bark, skitter over her leaves.
Yet we are the mice that gnaw at her root
who labor ceaselessly to bring her down.
When the tree falls, we will not rise as plastic
butterfly spaceships, but will starve as the skies
weep hot acid and the earth chafes into dust.

CHILDHOOD IN MEXICO

from *Almanac of the Dead*

Leslie Marmon Silko

Yoeme had appeared suddenly. Lecha and Zeta had been playing with the other children on the long wooden porch. From a distance the twins had both spotted the rapidly moving figure no taller than they were, a black shawl pulled tightly around her face so only her blazing dark eyes were visible. They all felt the eyes examining them.

Instinctively the children had huddled over the sunflowers they had picked and were arranging in old tin cans. They had waited for the strange figure to pass. Out of the corner of her eye, Zeta had seen it was a very old woman, dressed in a long black dress and black shawl. She had whispered to Lecha the old woman was an Indian. At that instant the tiny figure in black had turned into their gateway and stopped. In a clear voice as strong as Auntie Popa's, the old woman had said, "*You* are Indians!" Zeta had never forgotten the chill down her backbone. Lecha had cowered closer to her. Their cousins had jumped up screaming and fled inside.

But the girls did not run because the old woman was laughing, and she was not very big, and they both were. "Don't beat me up!" She laughed some more. "Dumb girls! I'm your grandmother!" Zeta and her sister had never heard anyone talk the way Yoeme did. But they had heard their uncles and aunties discuss a certain someone. Zeta had overheard them wishing the old woman had died. The discussion had been how many years had passed since the she-coyote had run off leaving the smallest ones, Ringo and Frederico, sobbing and running down the road after her.

Yoeme's name often came up with the subject of cottonwood trees. Somehow the morning she had abandoned her children, the long

driveway from the big house to the mine shafts had been blocked by the huge cottonwood trees felled across the road.

Auntie Popa had ordered the others to lock all the doors and windows, despite the summer heat. Yoeme sat on the porch swing and talked to Zeta and Lecha. What she did not understand was how her own children, conceived and borne in pain, could behave so shamelessly to their flesh and blood mother. Yoeme had said "flesh and blood" so everyone inside would hear it. Popa screamed, but the sound was muffled through the window glass: "Run! Run for your lives!" The girls laughed with the old woman. They would not get rid of her, so the girls should not worry. Yoeme could not be stopped. See? Already, she had the two of them on her side. If she wanted water, it was right there. She reached for a can full of sunflowers and drank the water. Both girls had squealed, and the windows of the house were crowded with suspicious, sweating faces. Yoeme was back and there was nothing any of them could do to get rid of her. Yoeme had slept on the porch glider until the winter rains came, and then she moved into the old cook-shed behind the big house.

Late at night Zeta had awakened to loud voices in the rooms below them. Popa and Cucha wanted the dirty Indian out of there. Yoeme liked to lie to them all the time, but very quickly the twins had realized that what was important came true. The morons would not be able to drive her away from the big house, Yoeme told the girls, don't worry.

Yoeme teased the girls, telling them she had advised their mother to get rid of one or the other of them right away. Twins were considered by some to be bad luck. If she had been around then, Yoeme said she would have taken care of the problem. She had watched both girls' faces for reactions. Zeta had asked, "Me or her?" and Lecha had said, "You kill me when I'm a baby and they'll hang you!" which had caused Yoeme to clap her hands together and laugh until their mother had come out to see what was the matter. Amalia had already been ailing awhile when Yoeme had reappeared. Like the others, Amalia seemed powerless against Yoeme. "I was just telling them how I urged you to get rid of one of them." Their mother had looked away quickly. "You'll scare them talking like that," she said, but Yoeme had paid no attention. She had even coached the girls to ask Amalia who had given birth to her. Their mother had given one of her deep, hopeless sighs. "Yes, she is my mother, although I do not remember her well." Amalia had clasped both hands to her stomach because the pains had come again. The twins had jumped back in awe of the pain. Yoeme had told them the pain was actually a jaguar that devoured a live human from the inside out. Pain left behind only the skin and bones and hair.

Amalia had leaned back in the wicker rocking chair on the big porch and managed to tell them more. There had been a terrible fight. A fight involving big cottonwood trees. "She left you and all her other children and her husband because of trees?" Zeta had wondered if her mother's pain was also confusing facts. Amalia had not been able to do any more than shake her head at her twin daughters. And then Lecha had said, "No, it was because she is an Indian. Grandpa Guzman's family didn't like Indians."

"Who told you that?" their mother had asked them. "Yoeme, I suppose."

"No," Lecha had said. "I just know. Nobody likes Indians."

Later when the twins were less frightened of the old woman, Zeta had asked, "Why did you leave your children?" and Yoeme had clapped her hands together and cheered the question so loudly even Lecha had blushed. They knew their mother's accusation that Yoeme was a bad influence on them was true. "Our mother told us it was the trees, cottonwood trees," Lecha said. They had been sitting on the ground in the garden next to the house pulling weeds. Yoeme stopped the weeding and tilted her head back slightly and squinted her eyes. "Yes," she said, "trees. The fucker Guzman, your grandfather, sure loved trees. They were cottonwoods got as saplings from the banks of the Rio Yaqui. Slaves carried them hundreds of miles. The heat was terrible. All water went to the mules or to the saplings. The slaves were only allowed to press their lips to the wet rags around the tree roots. After they were planted at the mines and even here by this house, there were slaves who did nothing but carry water to those trees. 'What beauties!' Guzman

used to say. By then they had no more 'slaves.' They simply had Indians who worked like slaves but got even less than slaves had in the old days. The trees were huge by the time your mother was born."

"But why did you fight over trees?"

"Hold your horses, hold your horses," Yoeme had said. "They had been killing Indians right and left. It was war! It was white men coming to find more silver, to steal more Indian land. It was white men coming with their pieces of paper! To make their big ranches. Guzman and my people had made an agreement. Why do you think I was married to him? For love? Hah! To watch, to make sure he kept the agreement."

But Guzman had only been a gutless, walking corpse, not a real man. He had not been willing to stand up to other white men streaming into the country. "He was always saying he only wanted to 'get along.'" Yoeme slid into one of her long cackling laughs. "Killing my people, my relatives who were only traveling down here to visit me! It was time that I left. Sooner or later those long turds would have ridden up with their rifles, and Guzman would have played with his wee-wee while they dragged me away."

"But your children," Zeta said.

"Oh, I could already see. Look at your mother right now. Weak thing. It was not a good match—Guzman and me. You understand how it is with horses and dogs—sometimes children take after their father. I saw that." And so Yoeme told the twins. It had been a simple decision. She could not remain with children from such a man. Guzman's people had always hated her anyway. Because she was an Indian. "We know," Lecha said. "We know that. But what about the trees?"

"Oh yes, those trees! How terrible what they did with the trees. Because the cottonwood suckles like a baby. Suckles on the mother water running under the ground. A cottonwood will talk to the mother water and tell her what human beings are doing. But then these white men came and they began digging up the cottonwoods and moving them here and there for a terrible purpose."

Cottonwood Trees

"I still see this," Yoeme said. "Very clearly, because I was your age then. Off in the distance, as we were approaching the river. The cottonwood trees were very lovely. In the breeze their leaves glittered like silver. But then we got closer, and someone shouted and pointed. I looked and looked. I saw things—dark objects. Large and small, swaying from the low, heavy branches. And do you know what they were—those objects, hanging in the beautiful green leaves and branches along the river?"

The two little girls had shaken their heads together, and when they looked at each other, they realized they knew what Yoeme was going to say.

Bullets, she explained, cost too much. "I heard people say they were our clanspeople. But I could not recognize any faces. They had all dried up like jerky." Lecha had closed her eyes tight and shaken her head. Zeta had nodded solemnly.

"So you see, when I decided to leave that fucker Guzman and his weak children, your mother was the weakest, I had one last thing I had to do." Here Yoeme clapped her hands and let out a little shout. "It was one of the best things I have ever done! Sooner or later those long turds would have ridden up with their rifles to hang me from the big cottonwood tree."

Lecha and Zeta had looked in the direction the old woman pointed in the yard near the house. Only a giant white stump remained. "What happened to the big tree?" Zeta wanted to know.

Yoeme had waited until Guzman had gone off to buy mules in Morelos, and then she had ordered the gardeners to get to work with axes. At the mine headquarters they had only cut down six of the big trees before the foreman had called a halt. Fortunately, while the foreman was rushing to the big house to question the orders, the gardeners had been smart enough to girdle the remaining trees. Yoeme had paid them to run off with her, since in the mountains their villages and her village were nearby. She had cleaned out Guzman's fat floor safe under the bed where she had conceived and delivered seven disappointing children. It was a fair exchange, she said, winking at the little girls,

who could not imagine how much silver that might have been. Enough silver that the three gardeners had been paid off.

Guzman had later claimed he did not mind the loss of the silver, which a week's production could replace. But Guzman had told Amalia and the others their mother was dead to them and forever unwelcome in that house because she had butchered all the big cottonwood trees. He would never forgive that.

The twins were solemn.

"I did not let myself get discouraged. All these years I have waited to see if any of you grandchildren might have turned out human. I would come around every so often, take a look." They were on the porch now, and Dennis, their pinheaded cousin, the son of Uncle Ringo, was sitting on the step, eating his own snot. Yoeme waved her hand at Dennis. "They had all been pretty much like that one," she said, "and I was almost ready to give up hope. But then you two came."

"But you wanted to get rid of one of us." Lecha had let go of Yoeme's hand in order to say this.

The old woman had stopped and looked at both of them. "I wanted to have one of you for myself," she said.

"But you didn't get one of us."

"No." Yoeme had let out a big sigh. "I didn't even get *one* of you. Your poor mother was too dumb for that. And now do you see what I have?"

The twins had looked at each other to avoid the piercing eyes of old Yoeme.

Yoeme laughed loudly. "I have you both!" she said in triumph, and from the bedroom inside they could hear their mother fumble for the enamel basin to vomit blood.

THE LAST DIAMOND OF SUMMER

B.K. Loren

The sweet smell of columbine, lilac, and wild rose trickled through the spring air. My grandmother stood, in high-heeled shoes, on the very top of the makeshift pitcher's mound in the center of the green meadow that surrounded our mountain home. She ignored her tight, restrictive dress, bent slightly forward at the waist, squinted and nodded at our non-existent catcher, then wound up and released the pitch. It swooshed over home plate. With a swing and a crack, I sent it sailing like a rainbow over the meadow.

We played until the spring twilight was the color of honey and the crescent moon rocked in the dark blue cradle of two shadowed peaks.

"One more," I called.

"One more," she called back. The crisp sound of her voice cut the thin mountain air like the music of a river.

If I gave her a line drive, she caught it. If I sent a pop fly out to left field, she ran after it, high heels and all, and most times, she made it back to the infield in time to hold me at third.

That was 1962.

By 1963, she was dead.

Even if I had known that the summer of 1962 would be the last summer I would spend with my grandmother, I don't think that her memory would be any clearer than it is now. I inhaled every moment of that summer as if it were simultaneously my first and last breath. My grandmother's cheek, smooth and warm against mine when we snuggled up to chase away evening chill; the smooth scent of her perfume; the way her hands curved around a baseball in a way that mine had yet to learn; these moments make up my most vivid childhood memories.

As I grew older, I began to wonder about the connection I had with my grandmother. I did not know my mother's mother very long. She

never lived with us, and I can't remember ever spending the night in her house.

I do remember visiting her though. And I remember that she felt like a "buddy." She understood me in a way that I felt no one else did. My grandmother was the only adult who did not reprimand me for being so active and competitive. She played baseball *with* me. She understood why, when I was in ballet class, I liked to run as fast and leap as high as I could—instead of running *gracefully* to make all the moves look delicate and lacy. She slipped me a dime before each ballet class because she knew I hated to attend them—and she knew it made my mother happy when I did attend. Still, the palmed dime and the understanding nod when I had to do "The Flying Dutchman" over and over again did not really account for the impact she had on my dreams and memories.

Twenty-four years later, I sat in a restaurant with my mother. She had traveled from Colorado to see where, and if, I had made a home for myself in California. I had succeeded and it was great to share it with her; but it was not like my home in Colorado. I had trekked across those mountains on skis, hiked them in summer, climbed many of their peaks, kayaked the rivers that ran through them and biked their deepest back trails. I knew the sky and its birds, where they nested and when they migrated. That land was my religion. And now, I felt vaguely exiled. I could not return home and feel altogether welcomed because my father disapproved of my lifestyle as a lesbian—and my mother disapproved of his disapproval. Still, I wondered, occasionally, if she also felt a little ashamed.

So there, with a cheap restaurant candle flickering dimly between us, casting amber shadows across the table, I asked her.

"Mom, are you ashamed of me?"

I will never forget the look on her face. I had listened to my mother tell the story of losing her first child to sudden infant death syndrome, watched her bail my brother out of jail, and listened to her on the phone while she consoled her friends who were sick or dying. But I don't think I had ever seen her look so shocked, so hurt, as she did in that moment.

"Why on earth would you think that I was ashamed of you?" Her voice cracked.

"Well, I thought you might be ashamed because I am in love with a woman."

My mother paid the bill and walked briskly out of the restaurant.

"Are you angry?" I asked, following behind her to the car.

"No," she said.

"Where are you going?"

"Home. I brought something I want to show you."

At home, my mother pulled some old leather photo albums from her suitcase. Faded black and white photos were affixed to pages worn thin by time. I opened the leather cover and turned each page slowly, careful not to pull the paper from its tattered binding. Photos fell like autumn leaves into my lap. I held them individually. I recognized my grandmother, but I had never before seen her in this light. I looked from the photos to my mother.

"Your grandmother was like you," she said. "She lived with Margaret for twenty-five years."

I was silent for a long time. When I could talk again, I was only able to mutter, "What about Grandpa?"

"He was fine with it. He loved your grandmother, and she loved him. But they were not in love like Margaret and Grandma. Nonetheless, we were a family. We all loved each other and were very happy."

"And that's how you were raised, Mom?"

She nodded her head, then held my hand. "Don't ever think that I am ashamed of you."

A quarter century later, I finally understand the summer of 1962. I was bonded with my grandmother by invisible ties that, in her day, were unspeakable. But her love for Margaret, and for the rest of her family, was strong in the face of that silence. It endured, as we all endure. In a world that paves shopping malls over wildflowers, and superimposes false restrictions on the delicate terrain of our deepest emotions, we have learned to make safe places for what we truly love; we have learned to endure.

RIFKA, GRANDMA RAE

Aile Shebar

The ring I wear on my fourth finger was my grandmother's. My grandfather bought the diamond from the Hassids on 54th Street in New York City and gave it to her as a reward for bringing the family safely from Russia to the promised land. It had been more than a decade since he had left her behind.

I loved my mother's mother. When she made *kreplach,* she would roll the moist dough on the floured board, peel it off the rolling pin, and hold it aloft, stretching it outward. Then she would give me a glass to cut circles which we would fill, shape and seal. The meat pockets she would drop into a pot of boiling water or chicken soup; those made of pot cheese, egg and sugar, she would slide lovingly into a small skillet, richly lined with melted sweet butter. She served those with fresh strawberry preserves and a dollop of sour cream.

She made her strudel with sultanas and walnuts, dense and chewy, covered with *betlach*—the fine pastry leaves we call *filo* that are used in Greek *baklava*. She would stand in my mother's modern kitchen at the wooden board that pulled out above the silverware drawer, next to the sink, her legs spread apart the width of the tea towel cupboard below, making her body a platform of strength from which to work the dough. Her practiced hands would thin the sheets. She pinched tight envelopes around the filling, brushed them with oil and put the ropes of pastry into the oven, four rows the length of the cookie tin.

I learned to bake by her side, to intuit when enough is enough, or when more would elevate something ordinary into something succulent, extraordinary. She would take a nibble of this, a hint of that, and I would watch magic grow between her experienced fingers. She formed delicacies that melted in my mouth—*fluden, humentashen,* rich cheese *blintzes*—and tasted of my Russian Jewish ancestry.

In my childhood fantasies I saw my grandmother as a girl of the Russian steppes, black curls to mid-back, soft suede boots made for riding stallions, in rosy skirts, bent at the waist to greet a villager with outstretched hand. Rifka! The dark sister with the flashing eyes and the dancing spirit, a gypsy holding answers to secrets I yearned to know.

Years later I would discover that the steppes were south of where my grandmother was raised, but my romantic invention of her astride her nonexistent stallion, charming her admirers, never faded.

Her mother was a midwife, her father a Coan, a learned man who officiated on holidays when the rabbi was absent. When my grandmother was still young, she went with her mother to births and to tend the sick, travelling to dangerous parts of the *shtetl*, inside the city of Chemelnick. She watched and learned.

Once as a child of five visiting her Los Angeles apartment, I spent a night delusional with fever. I dreamed she let black cats in through the screen door to walk over my body, endless lines of them down the back stairs out onto Fairfax Avenue. My grandmother's face rose above them in the humid night air to calm me. "Grandma," I called to her, "please make them go away!" She stood at the end of the sofa where I lay, a shadowy figure against the dim light, her hands clasped in front of her bosom, keeping watch. She couldn't halt the cats, but she seemed to raise their feet so I no longer felt them. And then she laid her cool hand on my chest, a healing poultice that lifted my fever, and provided a loving antidote to my fear.

She made other miracles. When I was five years old and visited her the first time after she left New York, I looked out upon the city of angels from her porch and saw her image in the clouds, a sleight of hand trick her shining spirit performed on me. "Bubbe, is that you?" She laughed, but didn't confirm or deny it. On another trip, the giant spotlights of a Hollywood opening night crossed one another in a firework sky as we watched from the chairs of her second floor deck. My grandma swore she made the show for me, crooning "shana madela, shana punim," beautiful girl-child, beautiful face, rocking me in her arms.

Married young to a man who had already fathered two children, she

was carrying his third child when he left to seek a better life for them in America. He would make a living as a tailor, then a purveyor of fabric bolts and dry goods in Brooklyn before the Russian Revolution. He said he'd be gone two to three years before he could send for her and the family. A war broke out, the early days of the famous struggle between the Communist party and the White Czarist government, and it would be more than a decade before she would see him again. So that she and her family could eat, my grandmother baked loaves of pumpernickel, cultivated a truck garden of vegetables, picked and simmered the ready yellow cherries in huge vats for jam, and sold to the Red Army soldiers at cut rate prices her bootleg vodka which hung from steel garters under her skirts.

When the Cossacks swooped down on her village looking for Jews, my grandma Rifka and her sister Eta would hoist my mother and Eta's youngest in their arms, grab the other children and run for the neighbor's roof where they would hide until their persecutors passed. Now and then, a few soldiers would linger to refresh themselves inside the neighbor's kitchen on vodka, tea, or the good looks of the neighbor's seventeen-year-old daughter. They would pass the time making lewd comments or challenge each other to drinking duels while my grandmother and great aunt held a silent vigil above their heads.

My mother remembered one time when Eta's child began to cry. "My mother covered the child's mouth with her hand. I thought she would die that way." I asked her why she would think her mother might do such a thing. She continued with an embarrassed laugh. "I remembered seeing my mother burying what I thought was the newborn baby of a cousin who was reputedly 'in trouble.' One day the girl was pregnant, and the next day she was not. The day her belly disappeared, my mother dug the earth around the fruit trees and I mistook the swaddled bottle of bootleg vodka she was hiding from her neighbors."

"What happened to Eta's daughter on the rooftop," I wanted to know.

"The baby grew quiet in my mother's arms, yawned a few times, and fell asleep while she, in hushed Yiddish, recited pet names in her ear."

One day a distant relative, a young scholar running from the city pogroms, arrived to stay with the family. It was risky having him in the house in case the neighbors decided to turn in the Jew. They were Russian Orthodox people who were already hard pressed to hide my grandmother, her sister and their families when the White Army stormed through.

The young man hid under the kitchen floorboards by day and came out at night to sit at the table with my aunt, uncle and grandmother to eat. My grandmother took new pleasure in her daily life after he arrived, preening in his presence, using her flirtatious eyes, inviting him into her heart. He must have found more than vodka under my grandmother's skirts at night, until he was forced to leave, his security threatened by an unwitting neighbor who stopped by for a sociable chat.

When my grandfather first left Chemelnick, he managed to send a few dollars from America in the mail. Then the small relief stopped, and Grandma Rifka lived on her wits. Finally, one day, boat tickets and money for the trip to America arrived. My grandmother packed their few belongings and left Chemelnick with her three charges. Their escape across Poland was made during the dark of night, on trains, in grave danger from war-weary soldiers who teased and tormented my sixteen-year-old Aunt Frances with their drunkenness and guns. My uncle was seventeen, unarmed and unable to protect his sister. My mother, eleven and barefoot, hid in the folds of her mother's dress.

The family survived physically unharmed, but children no longer, to board the ship that carried them to America. By the time my grandmother reached her husband's arms, her name was no longer Rifka. It had been anglicized to 'Rae' at Ellis Island. Her age was incorrectly recorded, but true to an innocent vanity, she never changed the date.

Through the years of her resettlement, my grandmother buried two husbands: Herman, who claimed her from Russia and whose Hebrew name I bore, Chaya, for Chaim, meaning 'life,' and Bill. Herman died in an elevator after a car accident and a fatal stroke. Bill was a simple good-natured man who worked as a downtown L.A. parking lot attendant and newsstand owner. I called him Bill-chick for his beaky nose and he

pinched my chin, making poor jokes in a funny crow-caw voice. I loved him too, even with his cigar breath and stubby whiskers. He let me sell candy and gum from the parking lot stand and bragged to anyone who would listen about his smart granddaughter who could make the right change.

Sometime after Bill died, Grandma moved from her home in Los Angeles to my mother's ranch style house on Long Island. She spent her last days first in the Hotel Ila, a Long Beach nursing home, where her black eyes still spoke of the steppes and adventure. Then, as the moment-to-moment grip on her mind faded, she was moved to a small hospital where she believed the other dying patients were stealing her money. She lay in her final bed curled fetally, blissfully unaware of where she was. Perhaps she was re-dreaming her life, her courage and pluck in adversity, how she had persevered to live in America after all.

My mother took me to see her twice in that state, warning me that the tower of my childhood would not recognize me. She lay there, moaning softly, her sagging white flesh exposed. Her arms made an empty circle on the sheets, as if she had fallen asleep caressing someone who had slipped away. I climbed the bars and curled beside her. I put my hand on her shoulder and stroked gently the salted pepper hair, and whispered, "I love you, Grandma," hoping her inner ear heard.

She turned toward my voice and opened her mouth, I thought, to speak, to travel the long distance across the steppes to reach me, across ninety-six years of memories, through the impressions that breathed beneath her surface, to lay my name there on the hospital bed, to say *shana madela*. Then, without a word, she slumped into the pillow and closed her eyes. "It's alright, Grandma," I said, soothing myself. "I love you, Grandma. I am here."

This woman I loved, who put her passion into the pastries she made in that red and yellow formica and wallpapered kitchen on Evans Avenue, was dying. I held her hand and remembered how she had clapped my small hands together in floury delight, her eyes shining with pleasure, singing *"hotchkala, potchkala"* for my having been born.

I KNOW WHY THE CAGED BIRD SINGS
Chapter 5

Maya Angelou

"Thou shall not be dirty" and "Thou shall not be impudent" were the two commandments of Grandmother Henderson upon which hung total salvation.

Each night in the bitterest winter we were forced to wash faces, arms, necks, legs, and feet before going to bed. She used to add, with a smirk that unprofane people can't control when venturing into profanity, "and wash as far as possible, then wash possible."

We would go to the well and wash in the ice-cold, clear water, grease our legs with the equally cold stiff Vaseline, then tiptoe into the house. We wiped the dust from our toes and settled down for schoolwork, cornbread, clabbered milk, prayers and bed, always in that order. Momma was famous for pulling quilts off after we had fallen asleep to examine our feet. If they weren't clean enough for her, she took the switch (she kept behind the bedroom door for emergencies) and woke up the offender with a few aptly placed burning reminders.

The area around the well at night was dark and slick, and boys told about how snakes love water, so that anyone who had to draw water at night and then stand there alone and wash knew that the moccasins and rattlers, puff adders and boa constrictors were winding their way to the well and would arrive just as the person washing got soap in her eyes. But Momma convinced us that not only was cleanliness next to Godliness, dirtiness was the inventor of misery. The impudent child was detested by God and a shame to its parents and could bring destruction to its house and line. All adults had to be addressed as Mister, Missus, Miss, Auntie, Cousin, Unk, Uncle, Buhbah, Sister, Brother and a thousand other appellations indicating familial relationship and the lowliness of the addressor.

Everyone I knew respected these customary laws, except for the powhitetrash children.

Some families of powhitetrash lived on Momma's farm land behind the school. Sometimes a gaggle of them came to the Store, filling the whole room, chasing out the air and even changing the well-known scents. The children crawled over the shelves and into the potato and onion bins, twanging all the time in their sharp voices like cigar-box guitars. They took liberties in my Store that I would never dare. Since Momma told us that the less you say to white folks (or even powhitetrash) the better, Bailey and I would stand, solemn, quiet, in the displaced air. But if one of the playful apparitions got close to us, I pinched it. Partly out of angry frustration and partly because I didn't believe in its flesh reality.

They called my uncle by his first name and ordered him around the Store. He, to my crying shame, obeyed them in his limping dip-straight fashion.

My grandmother, too, followed their orders, except that she didn't seem to be servile because she anticipated their needs.

"Here's sugar, Miz Potter, and here's baking powder. You didn't buy soda last month, you'll probably be needing some."

Momma always directed her statements to the adults, but sometimes, Oh painful sometimes, the grimy, snotty-nosed girls would answer her.

"Naw, Annie . . ."—to Momma? Who owned the land they lived on? Who forgot more than they would ever learn? If there was any justice in the world, God should strike them dumb at once!—"Just give us some extry sody crackers, and some mackerel."

At least they never looked in her face, or I never caught them doing so. Nobody with a smidgen of training, not even the worst roustabout, would look right in a grown person's face. It meant the person was trying to take the words out before they were formed. The dirty little children didn't do that, but they threw their orders around the Store like lashes from a cat-o'-nine-tails.

When I was around ten years old, those scruffy children caused me

the most painful and confusing experience I had ever had with my grandmother.

One summer morning, after I had swept the dirt yard of leaves, spearmint-gum wrappers and Vienna-sausage labels, I raked the yellow-red dirt, and made half moons carefully, so that the design stood out clearly and mask-like. I put the rake behind the Store and came through the back of the house to find Grandmother on the front porch in her big, wide white apron. The apron was so stiff by virtue of the starch that it could have stood alone. Momma was admiring the yard, so I joined her. It truly looked like a flat redhead that had been raked with a big-toothed comb. Momma didn't say anything but I knew she liked it. She looked out over toward the school principal's house and to the right at Mr. McElroy's. She was hoping one of those community pillars would see the design before the day's business wiped it out. Then she looked upward to the school. My head had swung with hers, so at just about the same time we saw a troop of the powhitetrash kids marching over the hill and down by the side of the school.

I looked to Momma for direction. She did an excellent job of sagging from her waist down, but from the waist up she seemed to be pulling for the top of the oak tree across the road. Then she began to moan a hymn. Maybe not to moan, but it was so slow and the meter so strange that she could have been moaning. She didn't look at me again. When the children reached halfway down the hill, halfway to the Store, she said without turning, "Sister, go on inside."

I wanted to beg her, "Momma, don't wait for them. Come on inside with me. If they come in the Store, you go to the bedroom and let me wait on them. They only frighten me if you're around. Alone, I know how to handle them." But of course I didn't say anything, so I went in and stood behind the screen door.

Before the girls got to the porch I heard their laughter crackling and popping like pine logs in a cooking stove. I suppose my lifelong paranoia was born in those cold, molasses-slow minutes. They came finally to stand on the ground in front of Momma. At first they pretended seriousness. Then one of them wrapped her right arm in the crook of her

left, pushed out her mouth and started to hum. I realized that she was aping my grandmother. Another said, "Naw, Helen, you ain't standing like her. This here's it." Then she lifted her chest, folded her arms and mocked that strange carriage that was Annie Henderson. Another laughed, "Naw, you can't do it. Your mouth ain't pooched out enough. It's like this."

I thought about the rifle behind the door, but I knew I'd never be able to hold it straight, and the .410, our sawed-off shotgun, which stayed loaded and was fired every New Year's night, was locked in the trunk and Uncle Willie had the key on his chain. Through the fly-specked screen-door, I could see that the arms of Momma's apron jiggled from the vibrations of her humming. But her knees seemed to have locked as if they would never bend again.

She sang on. No louder than before, but no softer either. No slower or faster.

The dirt of the girls' cotton dresses continued on their legs, feet, arms and faces to make them all of one piece. Their greasy uncolored hair hung down, uncombed, with a grim finality. I knelt to see them better, to remember them for all time. The tears that had slipped down my dress left unsurprising dark spots, and made the front yard blurry and even more unreal. The world had taken a deep breath and was having doubts about continuing to revolve.

The girls had tired of mocking Momma and turned to other means of agitation. One crossed her eyes, stuck her thumbs in both sides of her mouth and said, "Look here, Annie." Grandmother hummed on and the apron strings trembled. I wanted to throw a handful of black pepper in their faces, to throw lye on them, to scream that they were dirty, scummy peckerwoods, but I knew I was as clearly imprisoned behind the scene as the actors outside were confined to their roles.

One of the smaller girls did a kind of puppet dance while her fellow clowns laughed at her. But the tall one, who was almost a woman, said something very quietly, which I couldn't hear. They all moved backward from the porch, still watching Momma. For an awful second I thought they were going to throw a rock at Momma, who seemed

(except for the apron strings) to have turned into stone herself. But the big girl turned her back, bent down and put her hands flat on the ground—she didn't pick up anything. She simply shifted her weight and did a hand stand.

Her dirty bare feet and long legs went straight for the sky. Her dress fell down around her shoulders, and she had on no drawers. The slick pubic hair made a brown triangle where her legs came together. She hung in the vacuum of that lifeless morning for only a few seconds, then wavered and tumbled. The other girls clapped her on the back and slapped their hands.

Momma changed her song to "Bread of Heaven, bread of heaven, feed me till I want no more."

I found that I was praying too. How long could Momma hold out? What new indignity would they think of to subject her to? Would I be able to stay out of it? What would Momma really like me to do?

Then they were moving out of the yard, on their way to town. They bobbed their heads and shook their slack behinds and turned, one at a time:

"'Bye, Annie."

"'Bye, Annie."

"'Bye, Annie."

Momma never turned her head or unfolded her arms, but she stopped singing and said, "'Bye, Miz Helen, 'bye, Miz Ruth, 'bye, Miz Eloise."

I burst. A firecracker July-the-Fourth burst. How could Momma call them Miz? The mean nasty things. Why couldn't she have come inside the sweet cool store when we saw them breasting the hill? What did she prove? And then if they were dirty, mean and impudent, why did Momma have to call them Miz?

She stood another whole song through and then opened the screen-door to look down on me crying in rage. She looked until I looked up. Her face was a brown moon that shone on me. She was beautiful. Something had happened out there, which I couldn't completely understand, but I could see that she was happy. Then she bent down and

touched me as mothers of the church "lay hands on the sick and afflicted," and I quieted.

"Go wash your face, Sister." And she went behind the candy counter and hummed, "Glory, glory, hallelujah, when I lay my burden down."

I threw the well water on my face and used the weekday handkerchief to blow my nose. Whatever the contest had been out front, I knew Momma had won.

I took the rake back to the front yard. The smudged footprints were easy to erase. I worked for a long time on my new design and laid the rake behind the wash pot. When I came back in the Store, I took Momma's hand and we both walked outside to look at the pattern.

It was a large heart with lots of hearts growing smaller inside, and piercing from the outside rim to the smallest heart was an arrow. Momma said, "Sister, that's right pretty." Then she turned back to the Store and resumed, "Glory, glory, hallelujah, when I lay my burden down."

GRANDMOTHER

Lisa Williams

I.

I imagine three men
standing on the shore
of the Volga River.
It is dusk.
Sun slices into waves,
and they are laughing,
as she floats past them,
her blood mixing with water.

Her crime was a semitic face,
and a body warm,
holding secrets they longed to understand.

You were only sixteen,
Grandmother,
when you arrived to the shores
of America,
alone,
with the scar of your mother's murder
in your breasts.
I see you in your black high heels
and threaded shawl on the dock
peering at figures passing quickly,
startled by this land
of steel and brass.

II.

My mother tells me,
you were always old,
Grandmother,
even as you bore three children,
making your way each day
to the market,
feeding mouths open and needing you.
Your home was always by the ocean,
watching waves.
Sometimes as night descended,
you could hear the water weeping endlessly.

My mother tells me,
your hands shook in the evening,
as you sat rocking,
weaving your life into threaded wool.

My mother tells me,
she bought orange curtains,
placed flowers on the table
to ease the shame
she felt for worn wooden floors,
pain strewn like clothing
throughout the rooms.

III.

I remember the scent of meatballs
drifting past doors.
I ran to the kitchen,
where you stood

stirring the old steel pot
stained with grease.
"It will be good,
have a little taste,"
as the spoon glided into my mouth.

You tell me now,
"a mother is a precious thing,
Lizanka.
You need her when you are very young
and very old."

Your hands are trembling,
and your face is wrinkled
delicately.
The white hair on your cheek
quivers as you sleep,
Grandmother.

DANCING THE RAIN DANCE WITH NANA

Serena Makofsky

Nana swore like a sailor and flung backgammon pieces at Papa. One careened off his head and chipped the kitchen window but she kept pitching the brown and white discs at him until her supply was depleted. She doesn't like losing to him, but she always lets her granddaughters win. I creamed her at Canasta the night after my dog died.

Papa stormed out of the kitchen and Nana busily began hiding the dice in the arrangement of snapdragons on the center of the table. She's the one who introduced me to snapdragons when we walked through her backyard of wildflowers. The dragons astonished me with their color. I sat in the murky dirt, surrounded by strange and exotic blooms, my pinky inside a hungry dragon's garish mouth, feeling grand evil about to happen. Nana told me years later that among the snapdragons she had discovered and cultivated an odd plant. When they had first moved into the house they saw it and couldn't identify it. Much time passed before Papa got the *Encyclopedia Britannica* down off the shelf and figured out they were growing marijuana in their backyard.

There's a photograph of Nana in a Lucille Ball kind of dress and her hair is spilling down, thick, dark, loose, curly, and that's when I see I am her. We both have hair like our souls, lively and unsettled.

Nana had just turned thirteen when her father died. She got a job cleaning chicken houses to help the family get by. Her Mama would make chocolate that Nana and her sisters could sell at the local college. About a year later, Mama and her daughters started selling bootleg liquor to make ends meet. The night the cops came, Mama was out of town and Nana and her sisters had to shake a leg, throwing bottles of moonshine into the bathtub. Even though the liquor was drained from its incriminating bottles and jugs by the time the police reached the bathroom, they still hauled Nana off to the station where she spent the

night. Lack of evidence saved the family from further repercussions.

One of Nana's pastimes was to go out on the town with her Cherokee boyfriend. He would drive her to the edge of the city limits on the weekends to a place where the tribe held rain dances. The way she tells it, he'd join the circle of dancers and she'd stand on the sidelines, dancing with herself and chanting along with the group, "bum bum bum bum bum."

She never graduated from junior high, grew up surrounded by illness and poverty. Maybe she looked up at the stars the way I do. The same stars that followed her, along with the moon, planets and constellations, as she hopped onto the back of a motorcycle and headed for Fresno, California. No need for maps; when the motorcycle stopped, she kept going, jumping a few trains to get out West.

She got hold of a car and buzzed around Fresno's streets without a driver's license—she had learned to drive back in Wynnewood when she stole a boyfriend's Model T, careening and bumping down the road, motor sputtering, stopping, jerking her back and forth until her boyfriend, running after her as she zigzagged through town, managed to catch up with the car, leapt into the passenger side and took control of the wheel.

How did she become this softer, quieter person? Sometimes resigned and disappointed? Like when she wrote a poem, "I have no dreams, I left them by the streams."

She sees herself as a victim of her era when there were fewer options for women, especially those with a wild spirit and freedom in their eyes. I look at her and see success and inspiration. Her life is something I wish to touch, attempting to as I write, grabbing for a piece of her nomadic spirit. She curses her lack of choice, but, with all my options, I have never sold moonshine, danced a rain dance, felt the breeze in my hair as I wrapped my knees around a Harley, experienced the momentary flight as I jumped that boxcar, been a warrior, a goddess, free enough to later feel constrained.

SCRIM-SHAW

Tara L. Masih

It was a promise of womanhood to come, my grandmother's purse. Basketlike, in that style that was fashionable during the sixties. Only Grammy's wasn't a cheap replica of the Cape Cod fisherman's basket. It was authentic—a strong brown leather strap, worn soft from use, served as a handle. An oval carved from whalebone ornamented the lid; "scrim-shaw" was the word she used to describe it. The word rolled about my mind as the carved ivory ship rolled on the sea: "scrim-shaw." The word confused me, the way the first syllable scrunched up my lips, sounding like "prim," and the way the second syllable shot out, deep and strong, like a sea captain's voice.

I suppose the purse was first handed to me as button boxes and sewing baskets were once given to children—to keep them occupied. I was usually driven to intense boredom during long car trips, sitting in the backseat, between mother and grandmother. I would run through my small repertoire of nursery rhymes *a cappella,* play "I See the Color" until I'd used up every color within the Toronado's maroon leather interior, then fight with my younger brother, who sat in front of me on the armrest.

Grammy's purse was a welcome diversion. The contents, as I rummaged, were always the same. Yet I examined each object as if seeing it with new eyes. Her perfume, Wicked Wahine, permanently embedded itself amongst the basket weave and embroidered handkerchiefs and gloves. Her gloves were black, with long fingers, their only decoration a gold buckle at the wrist. When I slipped them on their softness enveloped my hands. The ends hung limply, dripping black from my fingertips. With an imagined diamond cluster on the outside of one gloved finger, I was Audrey Hepburn in "Roman Holiday," proffering my hand to Gregory Peck.

My grandmother, the elegant dame, smoked Eve cigarettes. The name conjured up the forbidden and the sensual. I would take one out, slip it between my fingers, the roundness a novelty, a privilege of age. They were a source of fascination, with appliqued wreaths of colorful flowers around the band.

Her lipstick, in a gold casing, twirled up in that bright pink-red color that all my aunts wore—the color that was left behind on cigarettes and rims of china teacups. That half-moon of color enchanted me. When I saw an ashtray full of pink-red cigarette ends, bent to extinguish, I felt that here was what a woman was. No man left that behind, but a lady, revealing her right to be feminine. My mother, the next generation, wore no lipstick, and I thought her lips and cigarette ends and teacups lacked something of life.

My grandmother was beautiful and cultured. She was not "Grandma," but "Grammy," a child's version of "Grandmère." Grandmère carried a shiny blond head of hair that, when not in a classic chignon, hung to her waist. Her comb, tortoiseshell, was central to the morning ritual of combing out her hair. After one hundred strokes, she pulled the lost hair from her comb to throw into a wastebasket decorated with oriental silk figures. Sometimes I would take these strands of hair and rub them in my hands, amazed at their fineness, as fine as mermaids' hair must be. She carried the comb in her purse, along with extra tortoiseshell hairpins because she always lost her pins. I imagined them scattered all over the world, from Alaska to Africa, from Switzerland to India. Spare hair nets held her bun in place and if the net was unpackaged I would take one out and fit it over my head. I would need a darker one when I grew older— my hair was not gold, but a dull brown.

Grammy used little makeup, and said she'd never gotten a blemish in her life. She loved bathing in the sun and always looked tan and rosy. She did wear lipstick and considered eyebrow pencil a necessity, for she'd plucked all the hair from her eyebrows one summer when she was in camp (girls were doing it that year to copy the stars in Hollywood) and they never grew back.

Grammy's purse always contained a yellow box of Chiclets. It

seemed bottomless—I always got a white tablet to chew on, and I wondered at the day when I could buy my own gum, carry it around in my own purse, without first getting permission from my mother.

Her wallet was fat with credit cards and family pictures, mostly pictures of my mother as a child. I made Grammy tell me the story behind each picture in its plastic envelope, never tiring of hearing how my mother had hated her Shirley Temple hairdo, or how she'd looked like a princess on graduation day.

Her car keys were to me a symbol of freedom. The metal shapes had an authority to them, and the polished stone hanging from the ring further emphasized Grandmere's elegance. What would life be like when I could open my own doors?

When the family traveled overseas, American dollars would be exchanged for foreign currency, and there might be extra Wash-n-Drys or a map of the country, but all other contents remained the same. Her purse never changed. It was a constant in a world where I was rapidly changing—body hair, braces, blemishes, blushing cheeks.

As I have grown, the definition of "woman" has also changed, the "scrim-shaw" dichotomy in strong evidence. None of the symbols in Grammy's purse of her kind of womanly power were passed down. They've been replaced with a different kind, a power that comes from education rather than social etiquette, ambition rather than sexuality, equality rather than puppetry. I should be happy for this. Mostly, I am, but I sometimes feel that if I had a granddaughter, my purse with its address book, bus and train schedules, calendars, checkbook, and moisturizing colorless lipstick just wouldn't occupy her for more than a minute. Would a child really look forward to attaining these utilitarian means to a new womanhood? What history is there in a schedule? Would she lose that sense of traveling down mirrored hallways, of looking back and back and back at herself? For Grammy was the first woman I followed, rummaging through her life, looking for the destination in mine.

PEARL BELL PITTMAN
(1888–1976)

Jan Epton Seale

She lies 1000 miles away,
all life-support tubes removed.
She breathes in and out, day after day.
I think of her great pendulous breasts
like warm loaves of bread
on which I rested my head in the backseat
through Arkansas and Tennessee one summer—
now shrivelled, crawling under her arms
like little shamed dogs as she lies there.
I see her thighs, hairless,
one bound in a brace since it snapped
one day as she merely stood:
seven babies came through these posts
(the seventh she told me of
one rainy afternoon sitting in
a certain gray armchair—
I horribly fascinated over the dead baby's
perfect curls, the prettiness of his face,
Grandfather wrapping him up and taking him out back).

Her hands twist open jars
of pickles, tomatoes, okra, black-eyed peas;
they skin onions, pluck feathers
from steaming headless chickens,
flick pinches of baking powder into biscuit dough.

They pick about in the turnip greens
for her favorite piece of hog jowl.
Delicate now, the tough, stiff fingers
lift the canary's cage door,
set in the lid of crumbled egg yolk.
She has me come to see the two eggs
in the corner nest, "quietly so as not
to disturb the motherbird."
I see her great astounding Victorian body—
six-foot-tall bride with a sober hand
resting on Grandfather's sitting-down shoulder.
The wedding—a Sunday night after revival meeting,
a trip three miles in a buggy home to her house,
a sister going upstairs with her
to help with a white nightgown,
wide pink satin ribbon woven down the front,
how she trembled when her sister left her
at the top of the stairs,
how she righted herself with a small smile
when Grandpa, ascending, said,
"Why Pearl, you look so pretty!"
(She wouldn't tell me more.
He had been dead fifteen years that afternoon.)

I think of her as a seven year old
on a train three days and nights
from Mississippi to Texas,
women and children in the passenger car,
men two cars back with the cattle
and household goods.

Another trip later, much later,
her firstborn dying in her arms
for want of milk. She rode two

summer days in a wagon to exchange
David Lee for his cousin.
Home again with a strange baby,
fat and ready for weaning to the cup.

Now my Amazon grandmother
lies, a great broken continent,
a land over-grazed:
breast tumor removed, colon unobstructed,
cataracts frozen, skin cancers erased,
bladder dilated—all the unnecessary,
acting-up parts long since removed—
womb, tonsils, appendix, gall bladder.

I want to get in bed beside her,
warm myself against her massiveness,
hear the punctuating sucks and clicks
her tongue makes cleaning her teeth
of chicken bits as she thinks of the next part
to the story she is telling.

I want to line up like a paper doll with her,
staring straight ahead on a genealogy chart—
my mother between us holding our hands.

I want to pick through the homestead
in Indian territory
for corset stays, sachet bags,
her churn lid, next year's dahlia bulbs.
I want to tell her it is all right
to have lived thinking mainly about
turnips and egg custard, the neighbor's child
with polio, whether the road out front
will be oiled down today or tomorrow.

A part of me lies in her eighty-eight-year-old
death-ridden body.
A part of her walks in my thirty-six-year-old
death-ridden body.

Goodnight, my Amazon lady.
Thank you for my bones.

Many of us remember our grandmothers as having unique talents, particularly in such areas as gardening, baking and sewing. Some had other talents that were extraordinary, such as a musical or artistic adroitness. Because memory tends to condense and magnify, some of our grandmothers are remembered more for what they did than who they were. This is true especially for many whose contact with their family crones was infrequent and brief. A summer vacation or a holiday meal may yield vivid memories of flowers, baked goods or vegetables, or songs and games. For one granddaughter, her grandmother's gastronomic habits provided the perfect excuse for discovering the delights of rich, sweet, and delicious pleasures.

LEMON MERINGUE PIE

Carolyn J. Fairweather Hughes

I can still see Nana after every Sunday dinner
trying to divide her lemon meringue pie
into nine perfectly equal pieces.

Anticipation of its frothy sweet, slightly tart taste
hovered around our tongues like tulle on a ballerina's tutu.
And each of us dreamed of stuffing ourselves with the whole pie
instead of just our piece.

We watched every movement of the knife in her hand
as if it were a magic wand,
and sat as quietly as we could
so that she would not lose count
and have to start all over again.

"Now, let's see," she'd say. "How many of us are there . . .
one, two, three . . ." and her voice would trail off
as she drew imaginary lines on the crust.
Then suddenly, she'd smile and look up at us.
We'd hold our breath hoping she had not lost count.

Elaborately she'd hand out the first piece,
which, of course, had to be passed clear around the table.
Each of us held onto the plate as long as we could
before the next one grabbed it out of our grasp.

What we did not know then was that Nana was stalling.
She did not want it to go too quickly.

She wanted us to appreciate the hours
it had taken her to make that pie for us—
her body bent at an oblique angle to the dough
as she kneaded and rolled it out.

In the background, the TV blared soaps,
as she argued with herself about the crust's thickness,
whether the egg whites were stiff enough,
the lemon jelled just right.

And the flavor? She held the delicate confection
to her lips. It melted on her tongue.
Her eyes focused on a tiny speck in the linoleum
as she tried to decide: was it sweet enough
but not too sweet, perhaps, just a trace tart.

She'd pause every once in awhile to listen
to a crucial piece of conversation
on "The Days of Our Lives"
so she would not lose the story line
and could discuss her suspicions.

Finally, my long-awaited piece was on the plate before me.
I wolfed down the first bite as fast as I could.
By the second or third, I was lost in a cloud of meringue,
the taste heightened by a lemon so luscious it literally
caressed my tongue, and the crust full of a delicate flake
that did not crumble at the touch of a fork.

And each succeeding Sunday, I noticed,
this ritual took just a little longer.
We talked more as we lingered over that pie
like a film in slow motion.

Only now, after she is long passed,
and each of us have gone our separate ways,
do I know the only ingredient in her pie
that I ever dreamed about: the love.

CORDELIA MOELLENDICK

Amy Cooper

My grandma was the best playmate I ever had. Because of her I still have a love of games that has not diminished since my childhood though opportunities for Scrabble, dominoes and anagrams are few these days. I can still hear her shriek of indignation upon drawing the "q" in Scrabble or worse, the "double 9" in dominoes.

When she wasn't busy entertaining her grandchildren, Cordelia Moellendick was attaining a measure of success as a journalist. As food editor for the local paper, the *Parkersburg News,* Grandma had a gift for language and a queer turn of phrase that made her daily column, "Diary of a Housewife," extremely popular among the locals. She combined recipes, jokes, household hints, all from her very own personal viewpoint, and blended them into an informative, chatty mix with just the right touch of humor.

Most entertaining were her rather low-key descriptions of personal mishaps. "It doesn't do me a bit of good to listen while someone tells me how they make a certain dish. I have to get a pencil and paper and write it down and then I have to type it right away or my abbreviations are so puzzling I can't make out my own writing. Once upon a time I was writing down a recipe for cranberry salad and the lady said to use two packages of lemon Jello . . ., etc. I wrote it just 'two lemons' and days afterwards when I copied the recipe and put it in the paper a lady called to say that the two lemons made the salad rather sour but she thought it very good nevertheless."

Even though Grandma's schooling ended at the eighth grade level, that handicap did not deter her from pursuing a writing career. From the manual typewriter on which she hunted and pecked her way to local fame flowed monologues, short plays for church suppers, and "Aunt Delee's Letter," a weekly column which preceded and paved the way for her "Diary of a Housewife."

A naive country bumpkin, Aunt Delee was constantly creating trouble while simultaneously extricating herself from some previous dilemma. Figuring prominently in Aunt Delee's escapades were her long-suffering spouse, Ben Quill, and their adopted boy/hired hand, Oaty, whose lack of common sense was exceeded only by his tremendous capacity for edibles of all kinds.

"'Oaty,' I sez, 'what do you want?'

"'I wants my supper.'

"'Supper,' I sez, 'why this is breckfast.'

"'I know tiz,' he sez. 'But I ain't had my supper yit, and I'll eat it first, then I'll eat my breckfast.'

"And so he did, he et 5 biskits (and I cut my biskits with a pint tin cup), 9 griddle cakes, 4 sausage cakes, 3 cups of coffey with plenty of butter and blackberry jam to fill the crevices.

"After he got hisself on the outside of all this—I sez to em 'Have some more breckfast Oaty.'

"'No,' he sez, 'I ain't hungry nuff to eat my breckfast yet.'"

Aunt Delee was at her most hilarious, however, when she ventured out from her country farm to town. After visiting a city church with her cousin, Gracie, her impression of the choir music was unique: "When I gits back home I was a tellin Ben about the Antheme I heered. 'Whats a Antheme?' Ben wanted to know. 'Well.' I sez, 'if I should say the cows was in the corn, that wouldn't be an Antheme, but if I should say the black cows, the Brindle cows, the muley cows, the spotted cows, the cows, cows, cows, was in the corn, corn, corn, then that would be an Antheme.'"

As we were growing up, my cousins and I didn't pay much attention to Grandma's writing. To us a visit to her house just meant fun and good food. I'm sure it's the same today for the lucky family and friends who visit her in heaven. I envy them as they feast at her table on oven-fried chicken, baking powder biscuits, half-runner beans, and custard pie. I sympathize with them too, for as she regales them with some fantastic tale, I know they are unable to eat with their mouths closed.

PEARS

for Kathleen Bridgette Nestor

Mary D'Angelo

O, how you filled
my baby days with sticky
sweet-tasting pureed pears,
strained through the family sieve.
The yellow-skinned fruit
with the spherical base
and tapered top
that you would skin
with your sharp knife.

How we laughed
when the cat played with the peel,
pawing it through the air,
while I sat strapped
in the high-chair,
my mouth shaped in
the smallest O,
my eyes wider than the
years between us.

My mouth a hangar,
the spoon of pears a plane
that zipped though the air,
each swallow followed by a laugh.

How our memories linger in the air,
mingle with the smell of pears
strained for the
dark O of your old lips.

I was never as strong as you;
even now I find it hard to
take my turn and strain the pears,
raise the spoon to your mouth.

You were the one who told me
never to pick pears.
You said wait and they would
fall when they were ripe.
I used to stand under the trees
staring up at the pears
with my hands cupped
waiting to catch them
before they hit the
ground to prevent them
being damaged by the fall.

I touch your falling face,
feel your gentle breath
as warm as summer rain
caress my cheek,
I raise my eyes to yours,
wrap my hands around your
breath and hold on tight.

GRANDMOTHER'S NERVOUS STOMACH
(1913–1920)

from *To Begin Again*

M.F.K. Fisher

One of the fine feelings in this world is to have a long-held theory confirmed. It adds a smug glow to life in general.

When I was about five, I began to suspect that eating something good with good people is highly important. By the time I was ten I not only knew, for myself, that this theory was right but I had added to it the companion idea that if children are given a chance to practice it, they will stand an even better chance of being keen adults.

In my own case I was propelled somewhat precociously, perhaps, into such theorizing by what was always referred to in the family as Grandmother's Nervous Stomach, an ultimately fortunate condition that forced her to force us to eat tasteless white overcooked things like rice and steamed soda crackers in milk.

Now and then either Grandmother's stomach or her conscience drove her to a religious convention safely removed from us, and during her pious absences we indulged in a voluptuous riot of things like marshmallows in hot chocolate, thin pastry under the Tuesday hash, rare roast beef on Sunday instead of boiled hen. Mother ate all she wanted of cream of fresh mushroom soup; Father served a local wine, red-ink he called it, with the steak; we ate grilled sweetbreads and skewered kidneys with a daring dash of sherry on them. Best of all, we talked, laughed, sang, kissed, and in general exposed ourselves to a great many sensations forbidden when the matriarchal stomach rumbled among us. And I formed my own firm opinions of where gastronomy should and indeed must operate in any happy person's pattern.

A great many seemingly unrelated things can be blamed on a

nervous stomach, as ladies of the middle and late years of Queen Victoria's reign knew.

Here I am, for instance, at least ninety-five years after my maternal grandmother first abandoned herself to the relatively voluptuous fastings and lavages of a treatment for the fashionable disorder, blaming or crediting it for the fact that I have written several books about gastronomy, a subject that my ancestor would have saluted, if at all, with a refined but deep-down belch of gastric protest. That I have gone further and dared link the pleasures of the table with other basic hungers for love and shelter would outrage far more than the air around her, to be sure: kisses and comfort were suspect to such a pillar as she. They were part and parcel of the pagan connotations of "a cold bottle and a warm bird" or vice versa—wanton and therefore nonexistent.

The Nervous Stomach was to Grandmother and to her "sisters" in the art of being loyal wives and mothers of plump beardy men a heaven-sent escape.

The pattern was one they followed like the resolute ladies they were: a period of dogged reproduction, eight or twelve and occasionally sixteen offspring, so that at least half would survive the nineteenth-century hazards of colics and congestions; a period of complete instead of partial devotion to church, usually represented in the Indian Territory where my grandmother lived by a series of gawky earnest missionaries who plainly needed fattening; and at last the blissful flight from all these domestic and extracurricular demands into the sterile muted corridors of a spa. It did not matter if the place reeked discreetly of sulphur from the baths and singed bran from the diet trays: it was a haven and a reward.

In my own grandma's gradual but sure ascent to the throne of marital freedom, she bore nine children and raised several of her sisters', loaned from the comparative sophistication of Pittsburgh for a rough winter or two in what was to be Iowa. It is not reported by any of the native or transplanted youngsters that she gave them love, but she did her duty by them and saw that the Swedish and Irish cooks fed them well and that they fell on their knees at the right moments. She raised a good

half of them to prosperous if somewhat precarious maturity.

As the children left the nest, she leaned more and more in one direction as her dutiful husband leaned in another, toward long rapt sessions with the Lord. Fortunately for the social life of the village such as she reigned in, His disciples were hungry, young, and at times even attractive, on their ways to China or Mbano-Mbang.

In a Christian way things hummed during the protracted visits of these earnest boys, and everyone lived high, even my grandfather who took to retreating more and more lengthily into his library with a bottle of port and a bowl of hickory nuts.

As inevitably as in the life cycle of a female mosquito, however, my grandmother passed through the stage of replenishing the vessels of the Lord, as she had already done through ministering to the carnal demands of her mate, and she turned to the care of her own spirit, as represented by her worn but still extremely vital body. She developed protective symptoms, as almost all women of her age and station did.

There were hushed conferences, and children were summoned from distant schools and colleges for a last faint word from her. She went on a "tour" with her husband to Ireland and the Lake Country, but for some reason it seemed to do him more good than it did her, and while he pranced off the ship in New York wearing a new Inverness cape, she left it retching and tottery.

At last she achieved what she had spent almost a lifetime practicing for, and she was sent *alone,* with no man or child to question her, to some great health resort like Battle Creek.

There the delicious routine laved her in its warm if sometimes nauseous security. Duties both connubial and maternal were shadows in her farthest heart, and even her morning prayers could be postponed if a nurse stood waiting with a bowl of strained rice water or a lavage tube.

One difference from our present substitute for this escape, the psychiatrist's low couch, is that today's refugees face few gastronomical challenges, unless perhaps the modish low-sodium-low-cholesterol diet can be counted as such. My grandmother found many such chal-

lenges in her years of flitting with her own spare crampish pleasure from one spa to another. Certainly what she could and would and did eat played a vigorous part in my own life, and most probably provided an excuse for my deciding to prove a few theories about the pleasures of the table in relation to certain other necessary functional expressions.

Grandmother did not believe in any form of seasoning, and in a period when all food was boiled for hours, whatever it was boiled in was thrown out as being either too rich (meats) or trashy (vegetables). We ate turnips and potatoes a lot, since Grandmother had lived in Iowa long before it became a state. We seldom ate cabbage: it did not agree with her, and small wonder, since it was always cooked according to her mid-Victorian recipes and would have made an elephant heave and hiccup. We ate carrots, always in a "white sauce" in little dishes by our plates, and as soon as my grandmother died I headed for the raw ones and chewed at them after school, and even in the dark of night while I was growing. But the flatter a thing tasted, the better it was for you, Grandmother believed. And the better it was for you, she believed, the more you should suffer to eat it, thus proving your innate worth as a Christian, a martyr to the flesh but a courageous one.

All Christians were perforce martyrs to her, and therefore courageous, and therefore all good Christians who had been no matter how indirectly the result of Grandmother's union with Grandfather had to eat the way she learned to eat at such temples as Battle Creek.

They could eat her way, that is, or die. Several did die, and a few more simply resigned from the family, the way one does from a club, after the cook had served Grandmother's own version of white sauce once too often.

By the time she came to live with us—a custom most aging ladies followed then after their quiet withdrawn husbands, helped by gout and loneliness, had withdrawn quietly and completely—my sister and I had already been corrupted by the insidious experience of good cooking. Thanks to an occasional and very accidental stay in our big crowded house of a cook who actually cared whether the pastry was light or not, we had discovered the caloric pleasures of desserts. And thanks to an

open house and heart to the south of us, where we could stay for dinner now and then while mother was "resting," we had found that not all salad dressing need be "boiled" and not all fried things need be anathema. The mayonnaise: it was a dream, not pallid loose something made of flour and oil and eggy water. The pineapple fritters dusted with sugar: they were dreams, too, tiny hot sweet clouds snatched at by healthy children.

We soon learned, however, that to Grandmother's way of thinking, any nod to the flesh was a denial of her Christian duty, even to the point of putting a little butter on a soft-boiled egg, but although her own spirits as well as her guts may have benefitted from the innocuous regime, ours did not.

Fortunately, at least one of my grandmother's phases of development impinged upon another, so that when she felt herself hemmed in by ancestral demands, she would at one time and the same time, in her late years, develop an extraordinary belch and discover that a conference was being held in a town at least thirty miles away, one in which there was a preponderance of well-heeled as well as devout dyspeptics. She would be gone a week or so, to anywhere from nearby Oceanside to a legendary religious beach-head somewhat south of Atlantic City. She picked conventions where she could drink a glass of lukewarm seawater morning and night for her innards, and it made slight difference to her whether the water was of Pacific or Atlantic vintage. It can never be known how coincidental were these secular accidents, but they were twice blessed for her and at least thrice for the rest of us: she could escape from children and grandchildren into a comfortable austere hotel and we . . .

We? Ah! What freedom! What quiet unembarrassed silences, except for the chewings and munchings of a hundred things Grandmother would not eat!

No more rice water, opaque and unseasoned, in the guise of soup. No more boiled dressing in the guise of mayonnaise. No more of whatever it was that was pale and tasteless enough to please that autocratic digestive system.

She would start off, laced into her most rigid best, her Jane pinned firmly under the white spout of her noted pompadour. We would wave and smile, and as the Maxwell disappeared down past the college, with Father tall and dustered at the wheel, we would edge avidly toward the kitchen.

Mother would laugh only a little ashamedly, and then we'd make something like divinity fudge, a delicious memory from her boarding school days. Or if it was the cook's day off my sister would set the table crazily—ah, *la vie boheme*—with cut-out magazine covers scattered over the cloth to make it crazier, and I would stand on a footstool to reach the gas burners and create.

Of course there were accidents, too revolting to detail here. But it was fine to feel gaiety in our family, a kind of mischievous mirth, and at the same time all of us, even the small ones, sensed a real sadness that we could not share it with the short, stiff, dutiful old woman, eructating righteously over a dish of boiled carrots in a vegetarian cafeteria near her churchful of "sisters" and even "brothers."

It was magic always then to see the change in Father's and Mother's behavior at the table when Grandmother was gone. They were relaxed and easy, and they slumped in their chairs as the meal progressed. Mother would lean one elbow on the table and let her hand fall toward Father, and he would lean back in his chair and smile. And if by chance my sister or I said something, they both listened to us. In other words, we were a happy family, bathed in rare warmth around the table.

It was then, I am sure, that I began to think of the spiritual communion of the act of peaceful eating—breaking bread. It is in every religion, including the unwritten ones of the animals, and in more ways than one, all of them basically solemn and ritual, it signifies much more than the mere nourishment of the body. When this act is most healthy, most healing to the soul, it obeys some of the basic laws: enemies do not break bread and eat salt together; one communes with others in *peace.*

And so we did, now and then when I was young. We met as if drawn together for a necessary communion as a family. The fact that we were refugees from the dietary strictures as well as the gastric rumblings of

a spoiled stern matriarch added a feeling of adventure and amusement to those stolen little parties. We sipped and dawdled, and I can still remember that occasionally we would *all* put our elbows on the table after dinner and Mother would sing, or she and Father would leave and let us stay on to indulge in the ultimate delight, in our pre-teen years, of putting a cupcake into our dessert bowls and covering it with sugar and cream. What ease, what peace, what voluptuous relaxation!

At home without Grandmother, we gobbled and laughed, and more and more I began to wonder about the meaning of happiness and why and how it seemed to be connected with the open enjoyment of even a badly prepared dish that could be tasted without censure of the tasting.

I was puzzled, of course, for I could not see why anything that made all of us so gay and contented could be forbidden by God. I did not know then, nor do I care to recognize now, the connection between self-appointed moral judging and the personal hair shirt of physical subjugation, as my grandmother must have known it when she had to bear one more child and yet one more child because it was her Christian duty.

Now that I am much older, probably as old as she was when she first began to escape from her female lot by feeling dreadful pains throughout her Nervous Stomach, I can understand more of the why, but I still

regret it. We escape differently now, of course, and today Grandmother would consult a couple of specialists, and perhaps stretch out on an analyst's couch, and then become a dynamic real estate broker or an airline executive or perhaps even a powerful churchwoman, which she was anyway. But she would have more fun doing it, of that I feel sure.

Of course, there was a slight element of sin, or at least of guilt, in the delightful meals we indulged in when Grandmother was not there, and as always, that added a little fillip to our enjoyment. I suppose my parents felt somewhat guilty to be doing things that Grandmother frowned on, like drinking wine or saying openly, "This is delicious!" My sister and I had not yet reached the age of remorse: we simply leaned back and sighed with bliss, like little fat kittens, unconscious of betrayal.

I think that I have been unfair to my grandmother. I realize now that what I've written about her has made many people think of her as hard and severe. She was neither. She was never a stranger in our house, and she taught me how to read and write, and I accepted her presence in my life as if she were a great protective tree. This went on until she died when I was twelve years old, and all my life I have felt some of her self-discipline and strength when I needed it.

Increasingly I saw, felt, understood the importance, especially between people who love and trust one another, of a full sharing of one of our three main hungers, which are for food, for love, and for shelter. We must satisfy them in order to survive as creatures. It is our duty, having been created.

So why not, I asked myself at what may have been a somewhat early age, why not *enjoy* it all? Since we must eat to live, why not make the best of it and see that it is a pleasure, something more than a mere routine necessity like breathing?

And if Grandmother had not been the small stout autocrat, forbidding the use of alcohol, spices, fats, tobacco, and the five senses in our household, I might never have discovered that I myself could detail their uses to my own delight. If my grandmother had not been blessed with her Nervous Stomach, I might never have realized that breaking bread together can be nourishing to more than the body, that people who sit

down together in peace and harmony will rise from the meal with renewed strength for the struggle to survive. My grandmother, who was stern and cold and disapproving of all earthly pleasure, because that was the way she had been raised to think a Christian and a lady should be, would never understand how she taught me otherwise. I revolted against her interpretations of the way to live a good life, but I honestly believe that I have come to understand as much as she of the will of God, perhaps, as Saint Teresa said, "among the pots and pipkins."

And like my grandmother, I am apparently touched with the missionary zeal, the need to "spread the word"! At least, I *suppose* that is why I began to write books about one of our three basic hungers, to please and amuse and titillate people I liked, rather as I used to invent new dishes to amuse my family. I had a feeling it might make life gayer and more fun. A Nervous Stomach can be a fine thing in a family tree, in its own way and at least twice removed.

HEIRLOOM HOCKED

Sheryl L. Nelms

I always gathered
spring greens
with Gram

down by Mission Creek

we would climb
those steep banks
picking
dock
dandelion
lamb's quarter
sheep sorrel
poke weed
and nettles

using knowledge
handed down
from mother to daughter
from England and Ireland

now with Gram dead
and a mother who got too sophisticated
become uncertain
can't quite remember

how many times do I boil the poke
and was it the leaves or the berries?

CARRIE ADELLA

Valerie Kack-Brice

En route to Cleveland for a visit with her daughter and grandchildren in 1966, Carrie Jones had to change planes at Chicago's O'Hare Airport. Being somewhat overweight from years of cherry cobblers and fried chicken, and having traveled very little in her sixty-seven years, she found negotiating the distance between gates a challenge. After walking with two full shopping bags for about twenty minutes, she noticed a man ahead of her pulling a rolling suitcase. He looked quite dignified in his pilot's blue uniform.

"Hey!" she shouted at him.

He turned around and with some annoyance said, "Yes?"

She looked at her watch, then at him, and bellowed in her Southern drawl, "Near as I can figure from all this walkin' we must be per'd near to Cleveland by now, is that right?"

As usual with people who meet her, he was disarmed by my grandmother's humor and helped with her parcels to the gate. By then, he probably knew more about her than he wanted to know and had likely told more than he was accustomed to telling.

My grandmother never had a problem with asserting herself and she loved to laugh. During that same visit, she hiked her skirt up to her hips and danced a jig in our garage ("Actin' the fool"), kept us kids running for paper to record her Tennessee colloquialisms, and fed us mouth-watering apple pie. We were fascinated by her. She was an adult who giggled until she threatened to "bust a gut" and could entertain us for hours with her stories. For three children who had moved several times to follow my father's sales career, she provided a link to the past and rooted us to people and activities that made our lives more meaningful. We had history (or rather, *her*story!).

My grandmother, Carrie Adella, was born one of twelve in 1901. She grew up on a farm in Parrotsville, Tennessee, that her parents owned

and worked. They were poor, simple people, living in relative isolation from the rest of the world. Carrie married young, as was the custom in farming communities, and was widowed at seventeen when her husband died of the flu. He left her with a three-month-old baby boy.

Her second marriage was to a man twenty years her senior, with two teenaged daughters. Because there was steady work available in the lumber industry, Carrie traveled across the country by train with her new husband to settle in Centralia, Washington, leaving behind with her parents the young son she could not afford to take with her. (She never spoke of this.) Her new life was hard. She worked as a cook in a hospital while raising three more children. At thirty-six, she was widowed again.

Carrie married for the third time in 1943. Her husband, Wesley, remained a friend and lover until she buried him weeks before her own death in 1991.

Carrie Adella was courageous, hardworking, and strong willed. But her most memorable feature was her sense of humor. She could giggle until tears rolled down her rosy cheeks, and have everyone around her holding their sides from the pain of laughing so hard. I think she took pleasure in laughter partly because she required of herself a stoicism that never allowed emotional or physical pain too near, despite her last thirty years of excruciating arthritis, ulcers, and circulation problems.

There was a lot that was remarkable about my grandmother. She appeared much larger than her size. Some of this may have been due to her big bones, big ears, big feet, and extra pounds. Even her eyes appeared huge because of the thick glasses she had to wear after cataract surgery. Or maybe it was her pendulous breasts which she constantly threatened to throw over her shoulder when they were in her way. Her false teeth, magnified many times by the water they soaked in, looked awesome and frightening. Her clear, directive voice made her sound bigger. When she was in a room, everyone knew it and deferred to her.

What was most definitely big about her were her hands; swollen from years of work and arthritis, the skin stretched taut and shiny over her huge knuckles. She used those hands like batons when she spoke, to

enunciate, emphasize, and illustrate her stories. Sometimes she would just throw them up in the air as if grasping for divine intervention and cry "Lordy, Lordy, Lordy! Gosh A-mighty!" Then she'd giggle. (I think she got as much pleasure from her own antics as she gave to anyone around.)

Those hands were adept. She would scoop perfect portions of flour, baking soda, and sugar into a bowl and roll together a pie crust, biscuits, or a delicious batch of cookies. Cleanup for her meant washing her hands and rinsing a bowl. She could scrape a bushel of fresh corn off the cobb or wield her paper-thin paring knife through a chicken in short order.

When I visited and found I had forgotten my toys, she would surprise me with a rag doll fashioned of an old nylon stocking rolled in a ball for its head and covered with a cotton dishtowel, ribbon at its neck. Painstakingly she would draw a face with eyebrow pencil and lipstick. The doll always had crossed eyes or a look of surprise.

Later, I watched her hands as she deftly shuffled the pinochle cards, dealt a round, and ordered her suits. She had the best poker face, unless no one else was looking. Then she would flash me a look of disdain or glee, partner to partner, and cover herself with a buck-passing giggle and accuse, "Oh, that Valerie Kackle . . . !" as if I had been the one who cheated.

She worked the hardest in the garden. When I visited we worked the rows side by side, pulling weeds, and as we would pass by still another unfamiliar flower I'd ask, "And what is this, Grandma?" She always replied with the name of the flower, as well as who had given it to her and when. There were thirty years of perennials and treasured orna-mentals. I like to think of the delphinium, foxglove, poppies, columbine, phlox, and astilbe that grow in my garden as hers, because she planted them with such love in my mind, standing there beside her pulling weeds. She gave me a passion for the feel of dirt under my hands, the yielding of small green intruders, the packing of soil around soon-to-be brightly colored seedlings. She would lovingly cup each blossom with those big red hands and declare how beautiful each was. I am convinced

those flowers grew for her, each striving to be the most beloved.

When she could no longer work, my grandmother felt her life was over. She had been "taking care of things" since she was little. Besides the baby goats that she would dress in baby clothes and push around in her younger sister's buggy, making sure they got their bottle of milk, little Carrie was responsible for gathering the eggs from the henhouse. She hated this job. "I would beg my sister to go with me up to the henhouse. They was big old black gopher snakes that used to hang around there stealin' the eggs from the mother hens. Those dirty old black thangs thought I was stealin' their eggs and would take off after me down the hill. They was as big around as a jelly jar and four feet long. I'd run as fast as I could, screamin' for bloody murder all the way. My dad would try to kill 'em, but he always made me go back to collect the eggs. To this day, I cain't stand snakes!"

As her life got quieter because the pain in her back and leg intensified and her friends died, she would sit in her chair, staring out the window and tapping her fingers silently on the upholstered arm. I always wondered what pictures she was making in her mind and looked for a clue in the pattern she would tap out. She spoke less then and when she did it was sometimes a complaint about the pain that made her want to crawl out of her own skin and how because of it she wished God would take her.

Conversations were usually about food or flowers or who had come to visit, but they were never about feelings. This might have been because she had to be strong all her life, and strength meant never giving in to the pain. Perhaps she felt powerless to change what was, or crying made the hurt worse and did little good. I wondered sometimes, if she had allowed the sadness to speak, would the wail be heard in Spokane?

I never saw her weep. Not when her favored son or her husband of forty-eight years died. Her eyes might well up with the missing, then she would tighten her jaw, purse her lips, stiffen her torso, and change the subject. Suddenly we would be talking about the Tropicana roses or cosmos—as if they were the remedy she sought for all life's hardships. I learned from watching her that nature can heal a broken heart.

She did have anger, however. When Carrie Jones got mad, her tongue was sharp and explosive. As a child, I was afraid of her anger which often pierced the quiet of my play with no forewarning. I was scolded for playing on the bridge that spanned the creek (a most treasured spot for princesses, knights, and trolls) or admonished to stay away from the Temple Emmanuel steps, where I pretended to be a bride or devised ways to peek into the windows of that mystery. To disagree with something I might say, she would bellow "Bull manure!" If she didn't like someone (particularly her husband's brother-in-law) she would spew disgust: "That old goat! He's nothing but an animal! Just stands in the garden and eats his dinner right off the vines!" She was harsh in her judgment of improper behavior and unforgiving of laziness, greed, and dishonesty.

Carrie Jones also cared what the neighbors thought. She told me about a dream she had one morning. This dream was familiar to her; she dreamed it many times. "It's always the same. I'm standing in a crowd of people, waiting for a parade or something big to happen. I'm all dressed up, looking real pretty. I'm feeling kind of excited and then suddenly I notice that I don't have any shoes on. Those people notice too and then I want to just disappear. But I can't! I have to stand there in my bare feet. It's just awful!" She was quiet then and blotted her eyes with the corner of her apron. Poverty seemed always at her heels, and she probably never felt free of the shame and fear of it.

I think of what it must have been like for my mother to live in the shadow of this woman. Little nurturing, harsh directives, inattention. Carrie Jones was a survivor; she was unsentimental in the attainment of basic needs for her family. Consequently, my mother grew up a survivor too. Poverty forced her to leave home at fourteen to work for another family and eventually to beauty school. Her beloved father died during this time and his nephew, Wesley, remained in the house. My mother felt betrayed by the growing attraction between him and her mother. It must have been painful for her to feel at such a young age that she could not go home again. Yet, for her as for her mother, grief and loneliness were not something to be acknowledged or expressed.

Much of my adult life was spent in depression, fleeing from or working to heal emotional pain. I have a different relationship to loss now than my mother and grandmother did. I have had the luxury of living comfortably, with the time and freedom to permit my tears. From this vantage point I see that pain brings a gift of release, and tears wash away hurtful memories and unwanted pictures. In wailing the anguish of my maternal ancestors, I am starting to feel lighter, less encumbered. My joy and gratitude have become shrines to their struggles. And the ability to laugh is the greatest gift I could receive from my bigger-than-life grandmother.

COTTONBOUND
for Addie Rose Smith

Gay Davidson-Zielske

With some of August
caught in batting,
the piled lump of pallet
smells the way she did.

Tobacco, woodsmoke, slippery shale
Each layer a generation, another summer.
Hot, hootowl, heartripping cry,
and then the whippoorwill.

Cottonbound, snapping beans on porch swing
cracking rocks out of pockets in the hills
to show me "pretties."
Cottonbound, you glittered one night
across snowfields in Minnesota
Snow and cotton bound me up with you.

Next day they called to say
you had passed while padding
a quilt, "jist as natchrul. . . ."
"Fluid about the heart or gout," they said,
I felt you had not passed from that,
but from yearning to catch Old Time
on a line and sinker, draw him by a pincer,
match his eye.

You cached these crazy notions in the quilt.
Sunbonnet . . . flour sack . . . Sunday silk,
though your berry mind was not in it, but

Out uprooting hens and finding speckled eggs,
fretting barefoot where the milksnakes
crawl as thick as mud and big around as your ankle.

About if the booger man was real, then what—
and if Jesus hung that long, or if tickfever
would bring you down this year.

You "probly" knew, six hundred miles away,
I grew to you like a snail to its shell, or
a chameleon lizard to your well bucket, or
bachelor buttons to the clay.
You most likely knew my fear.

MAMMY

Gangaji

My mother's mother, known to all her grandchildren and anyone who knew her as *Mammy*, was a true southern paradox. While she might cry out in anguish, "You're going to town without your gloves?!", she could easily be found in her nightgown on a ladder painting the house. She was hardly ever without an extra-long cigarette dangling from her lips. Each night she would meticulously cover my hands in Vaseline and cotton gloves before I could go to sleep, yet her own nails were frequently torn and peeling. She insisted I condition my hair with Helene Curtis creme rinse, while her hair was often whacked off and different shades of blue. I remember her sobbing on Easter morning when I was five years old when she discovered I had cut off all the curls from my new permanent wave. She taped them back on under my new Easter hat. Later that same day she chased a pack of wild dogs away from her house with her bedroom slipper.

Everyone adored her. She was witty and droll without even a hint of cynicism. Each of her grandchildren was absolutely certain that he or she was the most loved by Mammy.

She and my mother were often at odds. It seemed a strange kind of love affair. Mammy was always giving, yet always wanted something of my mother's soul. My mother could be cold to her and quite verbally abusive. I suspect jealousy as the root of my mother's behavior, since every visitor to our house was sooner or later captured by Mammy's love.

When my father went off to the great world war (II), we lived with Mammy and Granddaddy. It was there I tasted the sweetest times. Benevolent matriarch, she scolded, punished, and sometimes even spanked, but with a touch of love. It was a joyful time, and without words, she communicated her pleasure in our reckless ways.

In later years, when she and Granddaddy fell on hard times finan-

cially and physically, they came to live with us. She was my pillar of unconditional love. In a childhood that was mostly unhappy, she shines brightly as the protective angel, the willing bosom, the continual voice of approval. In my own hard times with my mother, it was easy to find an ally in Mammy. In her presence I experienced limitless love; even when she was sick or suffering some aspect of her personal tragedy, there was always love. When this love was met with the insensitivity of my adolescence, her response was more love. Not a cloying, sticky, sentimental love, but a rambunctious, joyous, or sad, eternal love.

She is my teacher. She taught a love that endures regardless of circumstance. Although she died twenty-five years ago, her teaching is even stronger today. Both the purity and the fury of her love have never allowed me to settle for less. Her unspoken guidance has stayed with me always. Internalized deeply into my soul, her example has supported my spiritual longing when all the world denied it. Fierce loyalty is the central component of her loving example. She never spoke in a spiritual vernacular, yet her trust has pointed the way to a deeper spiritual experience for me.

From knowing her love, I have learned that once the heart has been pierced by love, there can never be a turning back or denial of this love. There can be anger, fear, and even despair, but all can exist under the umbrella of this true love. It is love that finally sees only ITSELF.

"In great moments life seems neither right nor wrong
but something greater, it seems inevitable."
Margaret Sherwood

NO TIME
LIKE THE PRESENT

Occasionally a particular moment irrevocably alters us
and may remain a beacon throughout our lives, serving to
prompt a certain quality in our own interactions, such as
kindness or modesty, fairness or honesty. For some granddaughters, these lessons are hard won. Sometimes such a
moment captures the essence of the relationship between
grandmother and granddaughter. Often a gem is unearthed
from the sharing of a single activity on a specific day.

THE TRUNK IN THE ATTIC

Bernice Rendrick

On rainy days, Sister and I
drag our dolls, heads banging
up the steps to the attic.
Grandma's brogue, thick
as cocoa climbs the well:
What are you scalawags up to?
Nothing, just playing, we chime down,
our truths crumpled
in layers of tissue paper.
We yank open the trunk
that houses Grandfather's ghost;
his picture and war ribbons are buried
below mounds of baby clothes,
a blood-red dress scattered with moth balls.
Our hands recoil from braids, curls
of hair burrowed like dead creatures
among shoes without mates.
We come to the bundle of letters,
open them and pretend to read
that Grandfather will soon come home.

We clop the length of that long room
in cloaks and tipsy parasols,
our dolls having babies,
going to cake walks, box suppers
and ending the long morning with us.
An old mattress becomes a casket.
I lie down on it while Sister

props up dried funeral wreaths,
at my feet, smothers my body
with a blanket the mice have nested in.
Wrapped in a dust cover, she sways
a carpet beater over my face, intones:
Oh, Dearly Departed you may now rise
and enter the Kingdom of Heaven.
After my resurrection we clatter
down to the warm oven and cornbread
and the folds in Grandma's skirt,
our clothes streaked with coal dust
and dirt she claimed
we'd brought back from the grave.

OBASAN IN SUBURBIA

Susan Ito

When my grandmother was eighty years old, she got kicked out of her house for leaving her nighttime *kimono* in the bathroom one time too many. I remember the day she moved; I was ten. I sat in the backseat of my parents' station wagon while my father loaded her things—they fit easily into three or four cartons. He wrapped her little black and white television in a white chenille bedspread and laid it on the floor by my feet. She sat next to me, looking out the window, with a Kleenex in her fist.

She was living with my uncle Taro, her youngest son, his wife and my little cousin Jenney, in the big pink house she and my grandfather had bought after the war. When Uncle Taro brought his bride, Michiko, down from Canada, my grandparents invited them to stay until their savings grew. They never got any savings. They bought a car, a big one with automatic windows. They bought a fur coat. They bought television sets for every room in the pink house, and when my grandfather died ten years later, it was clear that Uncle Taro and his family weren't going anywhere.

That was all right. Nana would have been sad if they'd left her alone in all that space. But by that time the house had filled up with their things, pushing my grandmother to the outer perimeters of the house. She slept in the attic, in a small room with a slanted ceiling. Even though she was tiny, not even five feet tall, she could only stand up in the center of the room. She took her meals in the basement, back behind the laundry room where my grandfather had built a small, second kitchen, a one-burner stove next to an industrial size freezer. Sometimes she rested her plate on the ping-pong table and watched the Lawrence Welk Show while she ate.

The rest of them ate above her, Jenney spilling her Spaghetti-O's on the linoleum floor. It was like a split screen television, America above,

and Japan below. Upstairs, they called themselves Ray and Lillian. Lil. I think Michiko chose that name intentionally, knowing that my grandmother would never be able to pronounce it. "Lil-lian," she tried to say, but it always came out sounding like "Re-run." Changing their names never seemed right, anyway. Once, my mother told me that Aunt Michi's mother up in Canada never knew she was calling herself Lil. To me, they were always Uncle Taro and Aunt Michi. Ray and Lil sounded like something out of I Love Lucy. But there they were, upstairs, trying to fit that suburban life around them. He joined the volunteer fire department. She gave Tupperware parties.

In the downstairs kitchen, my grandmother shuffled on the cement floor in her rubber-soled *zoris*. She washed the rice in the sink where Lil's nylons hung, dripping. There was a pantry down there, next to the enormous refrigerator. One shelf was designated for her food, the cans she carried in a canvas bag on the subway from Manhattan. *Kamaboko*, and the stinky yellow *daikon*. White fish cakes with the hot pink coating. I stacked the cans and cellophane packages, neatly, on her shelf, playing Japanese grocer with my play money. *"Ikura?"* I asked my grandmother. "How much?" "Two hundred dollar, please," she laughed. Her teeth clicked in her mouth, and she covered her face with the back of her hand.

After a while they stopped letting her talk to Jenney. "She won't be able to learn English," said Aunt Michi. "When she goes to school, people will think she talks funny."

Ray and Lil gave barbecues in the backyard, my uncle wearing a red butcher's apron. They couldn't keep Nana locked in the attic, not on weekends with everyone around, so she sat in the cool basement, rolling logs of *sushi* on little bamboo mats. I helped her with the *nori*, thin sheets of green-black seaweed. You had to toast it first, holding it carefully over a gas flame or a candle. Nana didn't mind when I burned holes in it. "Don't worry. It's a window for the *gohan* to look out." We arranged the sushi pieces on a big round platter, and brought them out to the picnic table. Nana put it down right next to whatever Aunt Michi had made, green Jell-O or fruit cocktail with little marshmallows in it. Michi would make a face when she saw the *sushi*, like it was something strange and disgusting, so none of her friends would eat it either. She didn't tell them it was the same thing she loved to eat when she was a little girl. But sometimes I'd see her, after everyone went home, and she'd be standing next to the refrigerator, popping the little *norimaki* in her mouth when she thought no one was looking.

One of the problems with the house was that it only had one bathroom. Aunt Michi made it clear that it was *her* bathroom, and that other people, namely my uncle and cousin and Nana, were allowed to use it, but only because of her generosity. There were rules. The shampoo had to stay under the sink, not on the bathroom ledge. All her knick-knacks had to be arranged just so: the pink yarn sweater with the dog's head that covered the extra toilet tissue; the porcelain mermaid whose tail spread into a soap dish. Wet towels had to be taken directly down to the laundry room, and put in the dryer, set to high so that they'd fluff up. Wet towels were ugly.

One day, I was sitting in Nana's room, and the window was open. Michiko was out on the back patio with Kit. Kit was their next-door neighbor with red hair, who smoked, inhaling and exhaling like an accordion.

Aunt Michi said, "Tell me, Kit, what's it like to have your own house?" They were sitting in matching white Adirondack chairs, balancing glasses of iced tea on the armrests.

"Lil, believe me, it's no picnic. I've gotta clean up after the kids, after Mister Air-Conditioner King, with no help. At least you get a hand around here!" Kit took another long puff, and then let it out. "I don't think Ray's mother is so bad. What's the matter, she pick on you?"

I leaned against the window screen, not breathing.

After a pause, I heard Aunt Michi say, in her low gravelly voice, "She drives me nuts. She won't speak English. She won't eat anything that comes in an aluminum package. She shuffles around in those damn zoris like she's Mrs. Buddha. Kit, that woman has been here more than fifty years, and she acts like she just popped up out of a rice paddy!"

Kit laughed. "So she hasn't learned to say the Pledge of Allegiance yet. I think she's cute, Lil."

Aunt Michi snorted. "Cute. She's a pain in the *oshidi*."

"What?"

"You know what I mean."

Nana, at eighty years old, was still making a daily commute over the Hudson River to Manhattan, where she worked in a curtain factory. More than once, I watched her wrap Band-Aids around her fingers, which sometimes got caught under the machine's running needle. Her nails were purple and scarred, and each finger pad was a callous, but she liked her job. The sweatshop where she earned less than minimum wage was a place to feel busy, useful, a place to gossip with her Chinese lady friends.

My grandmother signed her paychecks, "Sadao Kitayama" in a long, snaky scrawl, the only English characters she knew. Then she turned them over to Uncle Taro for the mortgage payment. He went to the bank for her and deposited them in their joint account, keeping the little leather passbook in the locked drawer of his mahogany desk. It wasn't the money that mattered to her though, it was the work. Crossing the Hudson each morning on the big silver commuter bus gave her a sense of confidence, knowing that she could maneuver through places that Michi was afraid to go. She wandered by herself through the alleys of Chinatown, picking up unusual vegetables, carrying them in a bag made of plastic fishnet. Every night she came home, prepared dinner quietly by herself in the basement, and retired to her room in the attic. There was no sound to indicate her presence except the soft lilt of Lawrence Welk through the floor.

The crime that committed her to solitude though, the final insult, was the kimono, indigo and white in a bamboo pattern. She kept hanging it on the bathroom hook and forgetting to remove it in the morning. It riled my aunt; she didn't want to touch the thing, so she would leave it there and seethe all day. By the time Nana came home from work, Michi's face was set in steel. Two words only: "Kimono, Obasan."

No one ever told me the details of how it happened, how the family split that summer, like a tree struck by lightning. I imagined my aunt and

uncle saying something to her about how there wasn't enough space for all of them. My parents offered up our spare room, told her she could move in with us right away. But Nana was too sad, and too proud to accept. She insisted that they help her find an apartment, something small enough to be rented on her paycheck. It was an old brick building, in the same complex where my parents had lived as newlyweds. There was talk of a legal battle, of my grandmother winning her house back, but she refused to do it. "Taro my smallest baby," she said, wiping her runny eyes. "No fight him with lawyer." She turned away from the pink house without a struggle.

After she moved, my parents and I drove to Nana's place every Wednesday night and took her out to dinner. It made me sad to see her whole life in such a tiny box, her studio apartment. One room held a miniature kitchen, a folding metal table which she used for meals, and to iron on. Underneath the window was her single bed, a plastic cube-shaped nightstand and a phonograph on a rolling tea cart. The bed was covered with the white chenille spread and two plain yellow throw pillows she had taken from my uncle's couch.

My father tried once, a few years later, to build a bridge to the other side, but it was already too late. He went to Uncle Taro's house and stood on the front step, shaking the quarters and pennies in his pockets. Taro talked to him from behind the screen door, repeating, "There's nothing to say." My father's effort collapsed like a thing made of old, hollow bones, and when he came back to our house that night, we knew there wouldn't be another try. He stood in the driveway and opened the door to the station wagon, and my mother and I got in. It was a Wednesday, fried chicken night at Howard Johnson's, and my grandmother was waiting for us.

MEMORIES

Ethel Barrymore

It must be understood that there was never any money anywhere that wasn't earned week by week by this whole family by the profession of acting; except by my grandmother's Arch Street Theater which she leased and managed for many years—sometimes acting but always managing. So it was in Philadelphia that she had her house, and it was unthinkable that her daughter's children should be born anywhere else. It was a command tempered by sense and quiet, unspoken feeling. That house was our home as little children. In fact, it was the only home we ever knew together. We were separated very early in our lives by various circumstances. Consequently, when we met later in life we were rather formal with each other and very, very polite. It appears this rather terrified observers. I remember Lionel telling me that a friend of his who was present when I dined with him once said to him, "My God! Don't you know each other?"

One might write about the child one was with the same freedom that a novelist creates a character. There is no fear of egotism, for the portrait is one of faint colors, and the incidents that crowd in on any small life are incidents of any childhood rather than of a particular child. I see myself a shy little figure against the background of a family group whose vivacity was that of my mother and father, whose stronger, darker, more frequent moods were those of my grandmother.

I have never met anyone who had quite the amazing force without effort that my grandmother possessed. Her supreme rule at the theater crystallized into certain ceremonials that marked her comings and goings. She would drive from home in her brougham, and when she reached her office she would go over books, listen to reports, sign documents, and inspect things with that regal manner which betokens state affairs. And as she rose to leave, it seemed as though a red carpet should have been spread before her. When, in later years, I saw royalty abroad, nothing was to surprise me—I had seen my grandmother.

To her the theater was never "show business." My grandmother would rise up out of her grave if she heard me use that word. She'd say "show—do you mean a circus?" and she would say it as if she were the Red Queen saying, "Off with her head!"

She used to have dinner in Philadelphia at three o'clock, a cup of tea just before going to the theater and perhaps supper or a cup of soup afterward. We called her Mum-Mum (with the accent on the last syllable), which was probably invented by Lionel, as he was the eldest. And my father always addressed her as ma'am—like royalty, which, I must say, she received with equanimity. I feel that she regarded him as a person, and as an actor, a gifted amateur. According to her, one didn't spring equipped for the fray from either the Inner Temple or the British Civil Service. My mother she adored, though there was never any demonstration.

Once when I was about ten Mummum took me with her on a visit to Mr. Joseph Jefferson at his house on Buzzard's Bay. The only part I had ever seen Mummum play was Mrs. Malaprop and always with Mr. Jefferson as Bob Acres. I used to think *The Rivals* was the only important play in the world. One evening after dinner Mummum and Mr. Jefferson were sitting on the porch, rocking and reminiscing, when he said, "Don't you think so, Louisa?" She said, "Yes. You know, Joseph, you are the only one left who calls me Louisa."

And I burst into loud tears. It seemed to me so sad. Mummum turned on me in amazed indignation, when I was saved by a voice floating across the bay.

"Come fishing in the morning, Joseph?"

"No, Grover. Mrs. Drew is spending a few days with me."

"Oh! My respects, Madame."

On the way upstairs to bed I asked, "Who was that fat man in the boat, Mummum?"

Then I really did *get* it. Apparently one did not refer to the President of the United States as "the fat man in the boat. . . ."

[After my mother died,] I joined Mummum, who had gone to live with my uncle, John Drew, at the Sherman Square Hotel in New York City. There is a terribly trite word but I don't know any other to use to express what happened then; suddenly I found myself a pawn—a very unimportant thing that gets moved around a lot. I did nothing at all because of my own planning or thinking. I did what I was told.

Of course, I was a little bit bewildered. Mummum had been the pivot of the entire family and now something had happened and all the values were different. There was no explanation, and it would never have occurred to me to ask for one.

Even today, I cannot tell why all this came about. It is a characteristic of my family that we never talked intimately to each other about important things—never. Today I think that this is rather tragic.

But at fifteen I did what I was told to do and quite happily. The new surroundings, the changes put me in a state of mind that was not quite a daze—a sort of suspended animation.

Mummum was still there, very reticent, a person of absolute enormous dignity and silences. She had a comfortable room and she was Mrs. John Drew, Uncle Jack's mother. But it was Uncle Jack's apartment, not her house. He was then the prosperous member of the family, a leading man at Daly's. . . .

Every morning I would go trudging from agency to agency, looking for a job. This too, had been decided for me and, naturally, I did not think of protesting. Put away (though not forgotten for a long while) were the dreams of living a life of music and of a concert career. Every day I tried to find a job in the theater and I could not.

Always the answers were the same, "Nothing today!"—sometimes with a pleasant smile, sometimes with a frown. Apparently belonging to a well-known theater family is a handicap rather than a help. I have never known why this is, but all my children have found it so and I certainly did.

Mummum was unhappy at being dependent for the first time in her life, although it was on her own son, and she was bewildered by my not getting a job—all very tragic for her because she had been such a

commanding person with everyone's life in her hands for so many years. But instead of drooping, her back seemed to get straighter and straighter as she gazed out over the sinister rooftops of New York. I felt so sad because I couldn't help. It was the beginning of a long life of wondering where money was and where it went after one found it.

[Eventually] I got a theater engagement with Sir Henry Irving in London and it must have been sometime toward the approach of midsummer when I felt a sudden urge to go home and see Mummum before rehearsal for the new engagement began. . . .

Mummum was [by then] at the Bevan House in Larchmont, quite alone except for Jack. I was very disturbed about her. She had no friends staying there. She used to sit on the porch hour after hour, day after day, looking out at nothing and I suppose remembering everything, occasionally reading little paper-back books that she brought down in quantities from her room on the third floor. I remember them so well, those paper-back novels with blue covers. I used to wonder if she was really reading them or just passing time, turning over the pages while she was thinking of her great and crowded past.

She would come down in the morning and stay down until after dinner at night because it was too hard for her to climb those two flights of stairs—reading, rocking, and thinking. I couldn't do anything about it then, with what was left of my borrowed $100, but I kept hoping that as soon as my wonderful ten pounds a week began coming in from Sir Henry, I could have her moved to a lower floor.

Mummum never talked about herself and it was hard to get her to talk about anything. I was sure though, that she was pleased that I had come to see her. And her observations of the hotel and the people and of Larchmont in general were witty and penetrating. She missed nothing that went on, although apparently unaware of anything.

She seemed pleased that I was going to play with Irving, but she said rather cryptically, "Can you always understand what he says?"

I spent a week with her and then sailed back to my new and wonderful job. I went to stay a week or two with the Spenders (he was the editor of the *Westminster Gazette*) in Cheyne Walk, Chelsea. The day

I was to start rehearsals at the Lyceum the cable came, early in the morning. Mummum was dead.

There was much to be done, cables to be sent. Uncle Googan was in Australia. Uncle Jack was abroad. Lionel was on the road. At Larchmont there was only Jack, who at fourteen had to face what I had to face in California at the same age (when my mother died). Luckily my great-aunt Hannah, the sister of my grandfather John Drew, came forward and attended to everything.

But I was late for my first rehearsal. The old *commissionaire* at the stage door said with terrifying solemnity: "Oh Missie, you're late!"

I flew onto the stage. There was all the company standing about and Sir Henry, sitting alone in the center of the stage looking at me under his eyebrows, very coldly.

I said, "Sir Henry, I'm dreadfully sorry to be late, but something terrible has happened."

Still looking at me under his eyebrows he said, "What was it?"

I said, "I just got a cable that my grandmother has died."

And his face, that beautiful face, looked up. He said, "Mrs. John Drew?" and I said, "Yes."

He said, "Go home, my dear. No rehearsal for you today."

That was the first of his many kindnesses to me.

I had a letter from my grandmother a week after she died, thanking me for having come to see her. It nearly broke my heart.

GRANDMA'S STERN EXPRESSION

Savina Roxas

The moment I first saw her, I knew she was related to me: stern expression, high brow, gray-blue eyes that didn't miss a thing, a composite of my mother and her sister, came together in my grandmother's face.

I met her when I was in the sixth grade. That may seem strange because in one place or another we never lived very far from her. But my mother, Rosina, had committed the unforgivable sin of divorcing her first husband to marry my father so Grandma, the matriarch of the family of nine children, declared Rosina off-limits after her remarriage to Peter D'Agnessa. Only one sister in the family, Louisa and her kin, continued to see Rosina, but kept it secret.

Then came the move to Clinton Avenue and 178th Street, around the corner from Grandma. The new avenue being short, and a block down from Crotona Avenue, the bus and traffic route, was a quiet place except when P.S. 57 released the many kids that lived in the neighborhood.

I wasn't happy about the move; it meant another new school. Always, I found, the math, spelling, history and geography were not the same as they had been in the old school I came from. It took me a long time to catch up and I ended up feeling like a dummy. Now in the sixth grade I was in my sixth school.

Mama had been sick for a long time before the doctors discovered what was wrong. Each time we moved it was to find a healthier place to cure her cough. Peter said, "Now that Mama is in the tuberculosis sanitarium she'll be cured. God willing, soon."

Three months after the move, however, it turned out that the walk to school was even more discouraging than the school. Mornings, Grandma made a habit of waiting on the corner of Crotona and 178th Street for me to come by. Her rigid, black-dressed figure, outlined

against the white brick wall of the building where she lived, loomed like a giant crow threatening to shred me to pieces, as I came up the hill. Over tightly drawn-back gray hair, she wore a fringed knit shawl which she hugged to her waist, arms wrapped in the shawl.

From that stern face came, "Good morning, Savina."

Of course, I responded, with half a curtsy, "Good morning, Grandma."

"How you do need correcting," she said. "Ankle socks in the middle of winter." Her mouth snapped shut like a turtle's.

"I'm not c-c-c-old," I said, and looked down to the crack in the sidewalk, and stepped on it.

"You'll get rheumatism in your legs," she bent over to feel my legs, clucking all the time. I backed away, didn't dare wipe the spittle from my face. "I'm late. I gotta go," I said, and ran across the street not looking left or right, my only thought to get away.

Other mornings her inspection uncovered dirty fingernails, a milk mustache, an unsuitably light jacket, and on and on.

I missed my mother and often thought of one cold snowy day when I came home from school. My mother greeted me at the door, took my hat, coat, and mittens to the closet and then we sat at the kitchen table near the coal stove to drink our hot chocolate. I felt I'd never again in my life be cold. Then she took the kitchen curtain, white ruffled organdy, from the ironing board and draped it around my head, tying it in place with a ribbon. Singing, "Here comes the bride," she held my hand and walked me slowly around the living room. Through the window I saw the gray clouds open to a patch of sky, all pink and deep rose, as though winter had ended.

The morning of what turned out to be one of the worst days I ever had in school, Grandma waited, her black feathers shining in the sunlight.

"God catch it," she said. "You're still wearing anklets." With a yank, she pulled off my woolen hat. "Why do you want to look bald? Why do you stick all your hair under your hat?"

I wanted to pull the shawl off her head. "I don't like my hair cut. I look awful." I tried to take the hat from her.

She kept it firmly in one hand and with the other she ran stiff fingers through my hair. "Why you've lovely black hair. And there's nothing wrong with a Buster Brown haircut." She carefully adjusted the hat on my head, back far enough so the bangs showed.

That morning I was late. With my head down I put my things in the wardrobe and went to my seat. Mrs. Clancy was already turning to the math problems on page twenty-two. I felt sick inside, like part of me was still down there with that mean old woman and I felt I'd never escape. I paid no attention to the math; instead I concentrated on what I could do to avoid the old witch.

Mrs. Clancy flooded the blackboard with decimal and percentage problems, then called on me to come up to solve them. I came up and just stood there; my head wouldn't do a thing for me. Mrs. Clancy stamped her foot on the wooden floor and in a voice both loud and heavy said, "If you can't do sixth grade work you'll have to go back to fifth grade."

On the way back to my seat, my face blazed, and my heart hammered inside my chest. That's when everything I was holding in since I started seeing Grandma finally let go. All of a sudden, I was crying in front of everybody. I put my head down on the desk and started hiccuping. I gasped and sniffled, and never wanted to come back to school.

I crossed Crotona Avenue after school, unhappy about everything. To my surprise Grandma was at the corner. My stomach did flip flops. She'd never been there in the afternoon before. I wished I was invisible. In her hand she held a small package.

"Here are some long woolen socks I knit for you."

I took the package and stuffed it into my pocket. "Thanks, Grandma." I flinched, waited for what she'd say next.

"Come, I want to show you something." She started walking up the street and I followed.

At the Crotona Phonograph Shop, about a block away, she came to a halt. In the store-front window, a slim young lady was demonstrating different kinds of victrolas. The outdoor speaker filled the area with music. The young woman tossed her dark Buster Brown hair from side to side as she moved her body in time with the music: "When the red, red

robin comes bob bob bobbin' along, along, there'll be no more sobbin'…"

I felt like dropping my books down to the sidewalk and tapping my toes. Mixed with feelings about music was the realization that I looked like the girl in the window.

I looked up at Grandma, glad to see her stern expression had softened. I'll keep its imprint on memory's eye.

THE WEAKNESS

Toi Derricotte

That time my grandmother dragged me
through the perfume aisles at Saks, she held me up
by my arm, hissing, "Stand up,"
through clenched teeth, her eyes
bright as a dog's
cornered in the light.
She said it over and over,
as if she were Jesus,
and I were dead. She had been
solid as a tree,
a fur around her neck, a
light-skinned matron whose car was parked,
        who walked on swirling
marble and passed through
brass openings — in 1 9 4 5.
There was not even a black
elevator operator at Saks.
The saleswoman had brought velvet
leggings to lace me in, and cooed,
as if in the service of all grandmothers.
My grandmother had smiled, but not
hungrily, not like my mother
who hated them, but wanted to please,
and they had smiled back, as if
they were wearing wooden collars.

When my legs gave out, my grandmother
dragged me up and held me like God
holds saints by the
roots of the hair. I begged her
to believe I couldn't help it. Stumbling,
her face white
with sweat, she pushed me through the crowd, rushing
away from those eyes
that saw through
her clothes, under
her skin, all the way down
to the transparent
genes confessing.

BREAKING UP GRANDMA

Marjorie Maki

The terrible twos stretched into the threes for me. An only child whose mother was ill and hospitalized a good share of the time, I was watched by various relatives. But I missed my mama dreadfully, and acted accordingly. Apparently the only one who could cope with me was my grandmother in Wisconsin.

Grandma was a big strong Norwegian lady who raised eight children and milked nine cows the day after each child was born.

Once when she came to take care of me in our small home on the east side of St. Paul, I proceeded to make her life miserable. When she tried to take me for a walk, I'd scoot ahead of her at surprising speed, leaving her to chase me on her fifty-eight-year-old legs. When she devised an effective harness, I plunked down on the grass in our front yard and yelled. When she called me to eat lunch, I'd squeeze under my parents' iron bed, pulling down the chenille bedspread, or hide behind the brown overstuffed chair in the corner.

It all came to an end the day Grandma decided to soothe me once more in our old black wooden rocking chair. She had patience and lots of love, so she held me in her arms and sang songs from her childhood by the sea.

I was not impressed. I couldn't get away, and I still didn't like it. I pulled tendrils of gray hair out of her neat bun, poked an inquisitive finger up her nose and jabbed her cheeks. Her blue eyes remained amazingly calm. Finally, I slipped my fingers into her mouth. Instantly the singing stopped, and she wiggled her jaw in a funny way.

My hand came out holding her false teeth!

Shocked, I stared at the ugly things, dropped them and started screaming.

I cried for an hour. In between sobs I would hug her and ask if she

hurt. I kept hiccuping, "I'm sorry, I'm sorry." She rocked me contentedly.

My terrible threes ended that day.

You know, people have to be treated nice.

They break into little pieces if you don't!

MARY NINA

Valerie Kack-Brice

She was the first one to teach me about guilt. That, of course, was only a small gift from this grandmother. There were other things like permission to follow one's heart, like she did to marry my grandfather, out of the tuberculosis ward, out of the convent. It wasn't a big guilt she taught me, just enough for a four year old to sting a little. Mary Nina probably weighed over three hundred pounds and on her small frame, she looked more round than a peach. I was fascinated by her form. It dominated my experience of her. More so than the porcelain madonnas she painted in sky blue and white lace. More so than the black 1932 Model T she drove to get eggs.

What I wondered one day when she cared for me while my little sister was being born, was what she wore *under* her big round black skirts. Surely they didn't make pink polka dotted panties like I wore in her size. And surely, the white bras my mother wore couldn't be nearly enough to harness those huge face-crushing breasts. Did she wear diapers like my little sister would wear? Being a clever four year old, I figured I was entitled to know.

I schemed to catch her unaware and called her to look out the window at some unimportant detail I had identified to distract her. I dropped my rubber doll and kicked it under the sideboard and naturally had to get down on the floor to retrieve it. This required reaching way under. I had to turn my head (so I could see up her skirt). I was scared and ashamed, and only glanced upward then grabbed the arm of my doll and quickly pulled her out. Once standing, to my dismay, I realized I didn't know what I had seen. There were folds of cloth under there, but no true, clearly defined form of anything that looked like panties.

Though what I later learned to be guilt was nudging at my consciousness, I waited a day and plotted another research expedition. This time, I attacked from below while she prepared the biscuit dough at the

kitchen table. Sitting under the table, I could feel the shame rising to my face but was compelled to finish what I started. Although she was still a stranger to me, I knew she loved me. That deserved some kind of loyalty.

Halfheartedly, the ball rolled out of my hands and rested against the edge of her shoe. Perfect. I stared at it a long time. My mind fought to connect that foot to the folds of . . . something which was connected to my grandmother, the peach. I don't believe anyone ever taught me that it was impolite to look under a woman's skirt, but somehow, I knew that what I was doing was wrong.

My ball rocked against her foot as she stirred and kneaded. I watched it roll away a little, then back again. I felt sad. Only later was I to understand that my wickedness was probably more about missing my mother and my fear about who would be coming home with her to take my place. Then, I only knew I hurt from having to harness my curiosity with the sting of betrayal. In my mind, what I was doing had gotten complicated too by my remembering that she had been a nun. What I felt was surely the pinprick of God's wrath.

I couldn't do it. I reached for the ball without looking up, and said, "Grandma, can I help you make the biscuits?" I could. We did. And until she died, I remained only slightly curious and then, a little jealous of the undertaker. He was a real stranger and knew more about her than I ever would.

HANNAH AND ALICE

Riki Moss

Frightened guests stumbled out of sleep and hastily crammed whatever they could into suitcases, shopping bags and cloth parcels. Clutching their valuables, they staggered out into a rain of burning timbers and ran ragged down to the edge of the lake where a series of old wooden rowboats awaited them. The few employees who felt obliged to save the guests stuffed them hastily into boats and told them to paddle fast. The shabby convoy pitched and hauled out to safety, egged on by the intense heat at their backs. The fire they fled was irresistible. Heads jerked up and down on the quickening waves; fragile in nightclothes, disheveled and shocked, they sat in little boats staring at the burning hotel.

Near the edge of the convoy, a small girl wearing bunny pajamas jammed herself under her seat. Her name was Hannah. From this position she watched her grandmother's silhouette so dark against the flames she imagined her to be already consumed.

❈

The hotel was only second-rate, but it was more luxury than either Hannah or her grandmother Alice had ever imagined. They had been brought there reluctantly by Olivia, Alice's only daughter and Hannah's mother.

Olivia had herded them into the kitchen, waited impatiently for Hannah to settle herself on her grandmother's lap, and then started pacing in front of them, her stocking legs stretching the slit of her tight red skirt, the heels of her matching shoes drumming into the linoleum. "Your father's gone away," she said. "To Washington. On a special mission."

Alice mumbled something in Russian, which Hannah understood as "to hell he has."

"Speak English, Ma!" Olivia whimpered. She sat down, crossed her legs, lit a cigarette and sighed. "I'm exhausted," she said. "I need to be alone. So guess what girls, you two are going on vacation."

Alice said, "*You send him away and now you send us. Devil.*"

"English! You drive me crazy."

Hannah closed her eyes. In her imagination, she made the floor open up under Olivia's feet and held her breath until her mother had disappeared feet first down the gaping hole. When she opened her eyes, Olivia was bending towards her, red lips primed for a kiss, her face coming close in a cloud of cigarette smoke. A fit of coughing seized her, but she managed to say, "You're mommy's best little friend, aren't you."

※

It was Hannah's conceit that she had been born into the wrong family. She remembers hovering above Brooklyn checking out possible parents who stood in pairs far below her, waving their hands. Olivia was there with her husband Bob, transmitting deep reproductive wishes with all the rest, distinguishable only because Alice was nearby.

Hannah could feel Alice wanting her. She clearly remembers hanging still in the air, held by the longing Alice had for her existence. Even though she knew Olivia would always be trouble, she never hesitated. Alice's suffering was irresistible. Hannah dove right into Alice's heart and Olivia's womb. Hannah's life was on its way.

※

As soon as Olivia had left them in their cabin, had kissed the air on either side of their heads with a brittle little smile, and disappeared with a wave of her red-nailed hand back into her car, Alice burped pleasurably. She reached up to open the plain plastic clip on her head and fine, silvery hair floated down past her shoulders.

"Oh boy, kid," she said in perfect English, "we are going to have some fun now." She sat down next to Hannah, pulled her close. "Listen," she said, "there's other kids here, there'll be lots to do. We can sleep

together in my bed, don't tell."

"Do kids bring their dogs here?" Hannah wanted to know.

Alice didn't answer her. She rolled her sleeves up and her cotton stockings down. Then she opened the valise, found a wrinkled playsuit and helped Hannah get into it. "We'll do fine without her," she said. "Let's go find some kids. You need kids, sisters, brothers, not so many dogs," and took Hannah firmly by the hand.

In no time, she found a group of women, a generation younger than her, with kids around Hannah's age. She offered to baby sit these kids so Hannah could have friends and also, so she could make spending money. The mothers were happy to get free time for themselves, and a boy and three little girls were left for Alice and Hannah.

As soon as they had been brought to the cabin each morning, Alice would bustle them all out into a nearby field which was filled with ripe berry plants. She offered four cents a basket and soon the kids were quickly picking berries. Each noon, they came back to the cabin and while the kids napped, Hannah and Alice made jam together. In the little cabin kitchen they boiled the fruit with sugar, poured the mixture into glass jars which Alice had managed to sneak into her valise, then woke their charges and took them back to the main lobby where their mothers played bridge. Most days, Alice managed to sell a few jars to the guests and employees.

At night, Alice would roll up her stockings, put her hair back in the tight bun and tuck Hannah into her own bed with the radio on and a book in her hands. With a gleam in her eyes, she'd go down the darkened path to the main hotel building, disappearing into the bright lights to join the nightly poker game.

Some of her poker partners were husbands of the women who were paying Alice for child care and jam. They must have been amused by this immigrant lady breaking into their game. She was a skilled player and they begrudgingly accepted her. Unrepentant, she took their money.

One night while Hannah was asleep in her cabin, the main gas valve in the hotel's big kitchen burst open. Gas flew on the breeze down the hall, and got trapped by a closed door. Eventually, some guest entered

the toxic room, bent down, struck a match and blew off the back of the white hotel.

Just as Hannah was jolted awake by a dull alarm and the stench of burning paint, Alice tore into their cabin, with a man whose pant legs flapped like wings behind her.

Strong arms lifted her from her bed. "Wake up, move faster!" the man yelled. They ran outside. The hotel rumbled as flames burst through the rooftop. People were fleeing in a ragged line towards the lake. Hannah, bouncing high in the stranger's arms, stretched her hand out to Alice who was running behind them, trying to keep up, clutching the man's jacket.

They were halfway to the shore when Alice stopped suddenly and yelled, "Wait!" She bent down and reached for something in the bushes to her left.

"What are you, crazy? Come on!" the man yelled.

People started pushing them from behind.

"Come on!" the man yelled again, then took off running.

Hannah screamed, "Granny!"

Alice caught up quickly. She had something in her hands.

"Take this, quick," she ordered. She handed Hannah a tiny white puppy. It looked as though it had barely opened its eyes. Its white eyebrows were scorched. Hannah held it carefully against her shirt.

She was put down on the ground and Alice took her by the shoulders, turning her around. They were at the edge of the lake. It was quieter here. Men had organized themselves into teams, bringing rowboats out of a boat house into the water and helping the people climb into them. The fireball behind them glowed softly on the water.

A man wearing a tuxedo seemed to be in charge. He ordered people into this boat and that. "Make sure someone can row!" he yelled. "Row, row, row your damned boats!" Somebody was laughing. Someone else was sobbing. A ball of flame raced down towards the lake's edge, a human form flailing in slow motion beneath it, clownish and clumsy.

Hannah shut her eyes.

"Is the doggy blind?" she asked in a whisper. "Can it see me?"

The man who had carried her down from the room helped her grandmother into a boat, then lifted Hannah down to her. He settled himself at the oars behind them. "It's all right," he said in a kindly voice.

Hannah squinted through her eyelids. She thought she had never seen anything so beautiful as this flame framing her grandmother.

The boat moved quickly away from the shore.

"Oh, my god," the man said suddenly. Hannah heard a splashing sound and when she looked around, he was gone.

Alice heard it too, and turned to see him slide into the water. She watched as he swam to a child struggling in the black water. The boat had started rocking violently. Alice began crawling on her hands and knees, trying to grab the flapping oars. Hannah slid down on the bottom of the boat to let her squeeze by. Her pajamas were instantly soaked. She wedged her back against her seat. The puppy squealed and tried to crawl up her chest to avoid getting wet. Its tiny claws lacerated her skin.

Alice reached the oars and looked through the gloom to see how others rowed. She worked the boat out into middle of the lake and, taking a cue from the surrounding boats, turned hers so that they were facing the shore.

The water was alive with flame.

Someone said, in a voice that sounded very near, "Look, the winds are getting wild." Then, another voice, which seemed to rise high with the wind, said, "it's getting rough out here."

The small boat began shaking. Wind whipped out of the shore, carrying with it burning embers, some large as fists. Suddenly, Alice bent over as if in prayer. A cinder fell on her foot. She screamed and tried to put it out with her other shoe.

Seeing that all the other boats had begun moving farther away from shore, Alice tried to row faster. Waves grabbed at her oars and their boat began flailing; the prow dove into an oncoming wave, got hung up in its curl and shuttered, rocking violently. Suddenly terrified, Hannah flung out both her hands to grab the railing. As she did so, the white puppy slid down her chest, then rolled into the puddle on the bottom of the boat. Helpless, she watched a wave break over the side and disappear,

sweeping out with it the tiny pup who rode without a struggle, its soft head drenched in foam. Just as she reached out to follow it, Alice's arms came around her.

At the end, there was just the two of them—a child wrapped in her grandmother's arms, drifting to safety in a small boat. Hannah would nurture this image for the rest of her life, alongside the one of herself racing into Alice's heart to be born. No matter what happened, no matter how the world appeared and receded, threatened to burn or drown her, Hannah would always feel the wrap of Alice's arms; would always understand her language when no one else could; would carry with her the taste of sweet jam, the smell of her grandmother's loneliness, and the certainty of salvation.

I LOST IT AT THE MOVIES

Jewelle Gomez

My grandmother, Lydia, and my mother, Dolores, were both talking to me from their bathroom stalls in the Times Square movie theater. I was washing butter from my hands at the sink and didn't think it at all odd. The people in my family were always talking; conversation is a life force in our existence. My great-grandmother, Grace, would narrate her life story from 7:00 a.m. until we went to bed at night. The only break was when we were reading or the reverential periods when we sat looking out of our tenement windows, observing the neighborhood, which we naturally talked about later.

So it was not odd that Lydia and Dolores talked non-stop from their stalls, oblivious to everyone except us. I hadn't expected it to happen there though. I hadn't really expected "it" to happen at all. To be a lesbian was part of who I was, like being left-handed—even when I'd slept with men. When my great-grandmother asked me in the last days of her life if I would be marrying my college boyfriend I said yes, knowing I would not, knowing I was a lesbian.

It seemed a fact that needed no expression. Even my first encounter with the word "bulldagger" was not charged with emotional conflict. When I was a teen in the 1960s, my grandmother told a story about a particular building in our Boston neighborhood that had gone to seed. She described the building's past through the experience of a party she attended there thirty years before. The best part of the evening had been a woman she'd met and danced with. Lydia had been a professional dancer and singer on the black theater circuit; to dance with women was who she was. They'd danced, then the woman walked her home and asked her out. I heard the delicacy my grandmother searched for even in her retelling of how she'd explained to the "bulldagger," as she called her, that she liked her fine but she was more interested in men. I was

struck with how careful my grandmother had been to make it clear to that woman (and in effect, to me) that there was no offense taken in her attentions, that she just didn't "go that way," as they used to say. I was so happy at thirteen to have a word for what I knew myself to be. The word was mysterious and curious, as if from a new language that used some other alphabet with nothing to cling to when touching its curves and crevices. But still a word existed and my grandmother was not flinching in using it. In fact she'd smiled at the good heart and good looks of the bulldagger who'd liked her.

Once I had the knowledge of a word and a sense of its importance to me, I didn't feel the need to explain, confess, or define my identity as a lesbian. The process of reclaiming my ethnic identity in this country was already all-consuming. Later, of course, in moments of glorious self-righteousness, I did make declarations. But they were not usually ones I had to make. Mostly they were a testing of the waters. A preparation for the rest of the world which, unlike my grandmother, might not have a grounding in what true love is about. My first lover, the woman who'd been in my bed once a week most of our high school years, finally married. I told her with my poems that I was a lesbian. She was not afraid to ask if what she'd read was about her, about my love for her. So there, amidst her growing children, errant husband, and bowling trophies I said yes, the poems were about her and my love for her, a love I'd always regret relinquishing to her reflexive obeisance to tradition. She did not flinch either. We still get drunk together when I go home to Boston.

During the 1970s, I focused less on career than on how to eat and be creative at the same time. Graduate school and a string of non-traditional jobs (stage manager, mid-town messenger, etc.) left me so busy I had no time to think about my identity. It was a long time before I made the connection between my desire, my isolation, and the difficulty I had with my writing. I thought of myself as a lesbian between girlfriends—except the between lasted five years. After some anxiety and frustration I deliberately set about meeting women. Actually, I knew many women, including my closest friend at the time, another black woman also in the theater. She became characteristically obtuse when I tried to open up and explain my frustration at going to the many parties we attended and being too afraid to approach women I was attracted to, certain I would be rejected either because the women were straight and horrified or gay and terrified of being exposed. For my friend theoretical homosexuality was acceptable, even trendy. Any uncomfortable experience was irrelevant to her. She was impatient and unsympathetic. I drifted away from her in pursuit of the women's community, a phrase that was not in my vocabulary yet, but I knew it was something more than just "women." I fell into that community by connecting with other women writers, and that helped me to focus on my writing and on my social life as a lesbian.

Still, none of my experiences demanded that I bare my soul. I remained honest but not explicit. Expediency, diplomacy, discretion, are all words that come to mind now. At that time I knew no political framework through which to filter my experience. I was more preoccupied with the Attica riots than with Stonewall. The media helped to focus our attentions within a proscribed spectrum and obscure the connections between the issues. I worried about who would shelter Angela Davis, but the concept of sexual politics was remote and theoretical.

I'm not certain exactly when and where the theory and reality converged.

Being a black woman and a lesbian unexpectedly blended like that famous scene in Ingmar Bergman's film *Persona*. The different faces came together as one, and my desire became part of my heritage, my skin, my perspective, my politics, and my future. And I felt sure that it had been my past that helped make the future possible. The women in my family had acted as if their lives were meaningful. Their lives were art. To be a lesbian among them was to be an artist. Perhaps the convergence came when I saw the faces of my great-grandmother, grandmother, and mother in those of a community of women I finally connected with. There was the same adventurous glint in their eyes; the same determined step; the penchant for breaking into song and for not waiting for anyone to take care of them.

I needed not pretend to be other than who I was with any of these

women. But did I need to declare it? During the holidays when I brought home best friends or lovers, my family always welcomed us warmly, clasping us to their magnificent bosoms. Yet there was always an element of silence. In our neighborhood, and surprisingly enough in our family, that was disturbing to me. Among the regulars in my father's bar, Duke's, was Maurice. He was eccentric, flamboyant, and still ordinary. He was accorded the same respect by neighborhood children as every other adult. His indiscretions took their place comfortably among the cyclical, Saturday night, man/woman scandals of our neighborhood. I regret never having asked my father how Maurice and he had become friends.

Soon I felt the discomforting silence pressing against my life more persistently. During visits home to Boston it no longer sufficed that Lydia and Dolores were loving and kind to the "friend" I brought home. Maybe it was just my getting older. Living in New York City at the age of thirty in 1980, there was little I kept deliberately hidden from anyone. The genteel silence that hovered around me when I entered our home was palpable. But I was unsure whether it was already there when I arrived or if I carried it home within myself. It cut me off from what I knew was a kind of fulfillment available only from my family. The lifeline from Grace, to Lydia, to Dolores, to Jewelle was a strong one. We were bound by so many things, not the least of which was looking so much alike. I was not willing to be orphaned by silence.

If the idea of cathedral weddings and station wagons held no appeal for me, the concept of an extended family was certainly important. But my efforts were stunted by our inability to talk about the life I was creating for myself, for all of us. It felt all the more foolish because I thought I knew how my family would react. I was confident they would respond with their customary aplomb just as they had when I'd first had my hair cut as an afro (which they hated) or when I brought home friends who were vegetarians (which they found curious). While we had disagreed over some issues, like the fight my mother and I had over Vietnam when I was nineteen, always when the deal went down we sided with each other. Somewhere deep inside I think I believed that neither my grandmother nor my mother would ever censure my choices. Neither had actually raised me; my great-grandmother had done that, and she had been a steely barricade against any encroachment on our personal freedoms and she'd never disapproved out loud of anything I'd done.

But it was not enough to have an unabashed admiration for these women. It is one thing to have pride in how they'd so graciously survived in spite of the odds against them. It was something else to be standing in a Times Square movie theater faced with the chance to say "it" out loud and risk the loss of their brilliant and benevolent smiles.

My mother had started reading the graffiti written on the wall of the bathroom stall. We hooted at each of her dramatic readings. Then she said (not breaking her rhythm since we all know timing is everything), "Here's one I haven't seen before—'DYKES UNITE.'" There was that profound silence again, as if the frames of my life had ground to a halt. We were in a freeze-frame and options played themselves out in my head in rapid succession: Say nothing? Say something? Say what?

I laughed and said, "Yeah, but have you seen the rubber stamp on my desk at home?"

"No," said my mother with a slight bit of puzzlement. "What does it say?"

"I saw it," my grandmother called out from her stall. "It says: 'Lesbian Money!'"

"What?"

"Lesbian Money," Lydia repeated.

"I just stamp it on my big bills," I said tentatively, and we all screamed with laughter. The other women at the sinks tried to pretend we didn't exist.

Since then there has been little discussion. There have been some moments of awkwardness, usually in social situations where they feel uncertain. Although we never explored the "it," the shift in our relationship is clear. When I go home it is with my lover and she is received as such. I was lucky. My family was as relieved as I to finally know who I was.

THE BUTTON BOX

Shelley Parlante

In the weeks of her dying
lying in the spare bed
in the spare room, my
grandmother Amie
knows what I know
already being three: the
importance of the
flat cigar box
whose lid shows a
Spanish lady
holding a blue fan.

I set the box beside
her, raise the lid, and
one by one she lifts
out buttons gathered
like blooms from
a lifetime of mending,
saving, sewing
her clothes, my father's
and my grandfather's.

She sets them in my hand,
lets me lay them in rows
red, blue, green,
big, little
soft, hard
on the bed

where she lies
languid in the
afternoons when
the house grows quiet.

Heavy in my palm she places
a square button,
dark blue with a stab
of reflected light. She
wore it she tells me
on a too-warm dress
arriving by ship
a missionary's wife
in India. And I see
India as blue-black ink, the
squat bottle and the
lid I must never unscrew
for fear of permanent
stain, the ruinous color
I now hold, safely, and
set in a row of blues.

I reach for a brass
button, bright, smooth, taken
she says from the
black coat my grandfather
wore as he fled
from an angry crowd
when his bad dog chased
a sacred cow. And I see streets
made marvelous by
black and white cows from the
dairy herd next door,
freed from their muddy paddock

running beside Indians with
tomahawks and balancing
on their horns halos of gold
whose shine I now
hold cool between my fingers
and set in the softness
of her blankets.

The afternoon darkens
over rows blooming
in many colors as
the sun leaves the pulled
shades. Her stillness then is
like a river entering its
delta, slowing and letting
fall all it has carried
so far: wood, pebbles,
bits of bone, gold,
gathering and shining
as we arrive in silence.

NATIVE ORIGIN

Beth Brant

The old women were gathered in the Longhouse. First, the ritual kissing on the cheeks, the eyes, the lips, the top of the head; that spot where the hair parts in the middle like a wild river through a canyon. On either side, white hair flows unchecked, unbounded.

One Grandmother sets the pot over the fire that has never gone out. To let the flames die is taboo, a breaking of trust. The acorn shells have been roasted the night before. Grandmother pours the boiling water over the shells. An aroma rises and combines with the smell of wood smoke, sweat and the sharp, sweet odor of blood.

The acorn coffee steeps and grows dark and strong. The old women sit patiently in a circle, not speaking. Each set of eyes stares sharply into the air, or into the fire. Occasionally, a sigh escapes from an open mouth. A Grandmother has a twitch in the corner of her eye. She rubs her nose, then smooths her hair.

The coffee is ready. Cups are brought out of a wooden cupboard. Each woman is given the steaming brew. They blow on the swirling liquid, then slurp the drink into their hungry mouths. It tastes good. Hot, strong, dark. A little bitter, but that is all to the good.

The women begin talking among themselves. They are together to perform a ceremony. Rituals of women take time. There is no hurry.

The magic things are brought out from pockets and pouches.

A turtle rattle made from a she-turtle who was a companion of the woman's mother. It died the night she died, both of them ancient and tough. Now, the daughter shakes the rattle, and the mother and she-turtle live again. Another Grandmother pulls out a bundle that contains a feather from a hermit thrush. This is a holy feather. Of all the birds in the sky, hermit thrush is the only one who flew to the Spirit World. It was there she learned her beautiful song. She is clever and hides from sight.

To have her feather is great magic. The women pass around the feather. They tickle each other's chins and ears. Giggles and laughs erupt in the dwelling.

From the same bundle of the hermit thrush come kernels of corn, yellow, red, black. They rest in her wrinkled, dry palm. These are also passed around. Each woman holds the corn in her hand for a while before giving it to her sister. Next come the leaves of Witch Hazel and Jewelweed. Dandelion roots for chewing, Pearly Everlasting for smoking. These things are given careful consideration, and much talk is generated over the old ways of preparing the concoctions.

A woman gives a smile and brings out a cradleboard from behind her back. There is nodding of heads and smiling and long drawn out *ahhhhs*. The cradleboard has a beaded back that a mother made in her ninth month. An old woman starts a song; the rest join in:

Little baby
Little baby
Ride on Mother's back
Laugh, laugh
Life is good
Mother shields you

A Grandmother wipes her eyes, another holds her hands and kisses the lifelines. Inside the cradleboard are bunches of moss taken from a menstrual house. This moss has stanched rivers of blood that generations of young girls have squeezed from their wombs.

The acorn drink is reheated and passed around again. A woman adds wood to the fire. She holds her hands out to the flames. It takes a lot of heat to warm her creaky body. Another woman comes behind her with a warm blanket. She wraps it around her friend and hugs her shoulders. They stand quietly before the fire.

A pelt of fur is brought forth. It once belonged to a beaver. She was found one morning, frozen in the ice, her lodge unfinished. The beaver was thawed and skinned. The women worked the hide until it was soft

and pliant. It was the right size to wrap a newborn baby in, or to comfort old women on cold nights.

A piece of flint, an eagle bone whistle, a hank of black hair, cut in mourning; these are examined with reverent vibrations.

The oldest Grandmother removes her pouch from around her neck. She opens it with rusty fingers. She spreads the contents in her lap. A fistful of black earth. It smells clean, fecund. The women inhale the odor, the metallic taste of iron is on their tongues, like sting.

The oldest Grandmother scoops the earth back into her pouch. She tugs at the strings, it closes. The pouch lies between her breasts, warming her skin. Her breasts are supple and soft for one so old. Not long ago, she nursed a sister back to health. A child drank from her breast and was healed of evil spirits that entered her while she lay innocent and dreaming.

The ceremony is over. The magic things are put in their places. The old women kiss and touch each other's faces. They go out in the night. The moon and stars are parts of the body of Sky Woman. She glows on, never dimming. Never receding.

The Grandmothers go inside the Longhouse. They tend the fire, and wait.

"Only one thing is more frightening than speaking your truth.
And that is not speaking."
Naomi Wolf

A WORD TO THE WISE

Sometimes, with age comes wisdom. These pioneering women were wise with skills and experience, and they were often able to share with us their intuition, nurturing, compassion, and personal truths. Often this occurred in a simple act of relating a story, teaching a lesson, or modeling.

In the following offerings, words brought hope and encouragement. The special way a loving grandparent spoke a child's name was soothing. Some words, sacred phrases, or secular advice conjured healing for spiritual or physical wounds. Other words became cues for listening well; what followed might change a life forever. For one granddaughter, a grandmother's words taught her to appreciate everyday activities for their simple truths and wise instruction. Two other women had the task of instructing their grandmothers, and were strengthened.

THE SOUND OF MY NAME

Dilys Morris

Over and over
I call her back to me—
her flowered bathrobe
with pink trim around the collar
glasses a little crooked
hair wispy white.
Scuffing blue terrycloth slippers
she turns toward me,
grasping the counter edge for balance,
and speaks my name
with more love than anyone
ever squeezed into one word.
Over and over
I listen to the sound of my name—
the memory of her, speaking my name.

CARRIE JAMISON WHITTAKER

Carolyn S. Mateer

My grandmother probably never left Huntingdon County, Pennsylvania, as long as she lived. Though I remember her as an elderly woman, stocky with a knot of grey hair typical of her generation, early pictures show a beautiful, but serious young woman, married at sixteen to escape the household of a stern, unloving stepmother. Whether that escape was to a destiny more, or less, painful, I am not sure. I do know that the geographical boundaries imposed on her were only limitations of experience, not of wisdom.

Her husband, my grandfather, was the town barber. She had probably expected more of him, since his father had been the editor of the county's leading newspaper and a respected scholar. Time would prove that, though he was a good man, he lacked his father's ambition or intellectual interests and had no desire to do more than run the simple shop where men came daily for a shave and kept their individual mugs on a shelf above the antiquated barber's chair.

Despite the hardship and penury, I knew early on that my grandmother was special; she always had time to wipe a tear, bandage a scratched knee, tell a story. I did not know that she was an artist, that her aesthetic sense was true and unerring, and that beauty, so hard to come by in her hardscrabble existence, was important to her very soul. She died when I was seven, yet my memories of her are strong and vivid— perhaps because they were formed during those years when, for a child, certain events become the leavening for much that is to come.

Her days were consumed with the elements of survival, feeding a large family, knitting their stockings, mittens and sweaters, sewing shirts for the men and dresses for the girls. A treasured photograph of her children, taken when the girls were in their teens, shows each in a filmy batiste dress with tucked bodices and high collars edged with lace, meticulously sewn on an ancient Singer treadle. Leisure time was an

unknown luxury, but she compensated by turning every daily chore into an act of creation.

In the evenings she was free to merge her talents with her artistry. Seated at the quilting frame illuminated only by lamplight, she stitched away on her masterpieces, quilts of intricate design and execution, crafted from an inner sense of spatial proportion, of symmetry and color. Her rock garden, painstakingly created by hauling rocks from the creekbed, was visual evidence of that same aesthetic gift. Occupying space sacrificed from the vegetable plot which provided most of the food, nourishment from the flowers was richer and equally sustaining.

As a child I was allowed to walk the mile from my home in the village to the white house in the country where she had lived for over fifty years. I knew she would always be there, hovering over a coal-fired stove on a sultry summer day. The kitchen always smelled of baking bread or herb-laden kettles of soup. Sometimes there would be preserves simmering on the back burner, and often rows of jars filled with the day's canning lined the old pine table that later seated nine or more for dinner. The quilting frame occupied a place of prominence, placed to catch the light from the largest window.

Self-knowledge is seldom sufficient to identify the circumstances which create one's values, but I know that one special moment with Carrie Whittaker is indelibly etched on my memory. We were alone in her cavernous kitchen after a family dinner. It must have been a gathering of some consequence, a special birthday or anniversary. The table had been set with her only possessions of any real value: a set of china passed down from some more affluent ancestor. Whether the dishes were Spode or Wedgewood, or simply the product of some local Pennsylvania potter, I knew they were valued beyond anything else in that simple house, and were perhaps the only things she owned of any material significance. Of far greater importance was the fact that she loved them. I had seen her hold a dish to the light to catch the play of sunshine on the blues and golds of the dainty floral pattern so typical of nineteenth-century dinnerware.

I was no more than six, hanging on her skirts, anxious for the table

clearing and dish-washing to be over so I could cuddle in her ample lap for a story and a hug. Eager to move things along, I carried plates from the table to the sink to be scraped, despite the apprehensive glances shot my way. The worst happened, of course. The vegetable dish slipped from my hands, scattering broken glass and bits of corn across the worn linoleum. I had an instant feeling of sharp inner pain, worse than I had ever experienced from a cut finger or a scraped knee. For the first time in my life, I came face to face with true anguish, guilt that could never be totally resolved.

For one long moment there was silence, broken only when sobs came pouring out from deep in my throat. She looked at me for an additional second or two, and then, picking me up and heading for the rocker in the window, said, "I'm glad you broke that dish; I was getting tired of it."

She died a lingering death from the stomach cancer for which there was little surcease in the 1930s. By then, I had forgotten the incident, or, perhaps filed it away in that convenient spot where things too painful to reconcile can be hidden. Eventually the dishes, too, were scattered, their existence little noted nor remembered. But the quilts hang in the homes of her great- grandchildren, worthy works of art and cherished memorabilia of a treasured heritage.

GRAMMA MINNIE

E. K. Caldwell

Slightly built
wiry
tough
smoldering eyes that see through
past the heart

white shining hair
braided
as she braided mine
tight
close to the head
till the eyebrows arch
and the eyes slant at their edges

whispering secrets
just between us.

sitting on the old couch
tucked in its corner
the smell of tobacco
she chewed
and spit in a coffee can.

and the sweets she loved
looked like watermelon
pink and green
and white
sugared coconut
always shared with me.

outlived all her husbands
would never say how many

don't cut your hair, girl
power in your hair
comes down through
and meets what comes through your feet
right in the middle of you
ok, gramma, I won't cut my hair.

burning medicine in the house
when the thunderers came
said be still and listen
and learn something for a change

said wailing wasn't bad
when it hurt too much to stand anymore
not good to cry too much though
makes the brain soggy

can't think clear then
have to think clear to get along, girl
the beat of the heart
clears the head
listen. hear it?
that's life you hear.

one day her eyes looked different at me
and then the doctor said,
Cataracts.
what's that mean, gramma
(The thick glasses scared me at first.)
means nothing—I can still see you
and don't go thinkin

you can get away with nothin.
ok gramma

and then they cut off her hair
and rain fell from her eyes
and I didn't say a word
about our secret
no matter how bad I wanted to . . .

but I still remember
don't cut your hair, girl
power in your hair
comes down through
and meets what comes through your feet
right in the middle of you.

ok gramma
I
won't
cut
my
hair.

REMEMBERING HONEYCAKE

Dawna Markova

When I think of her, even today, I smell bread. That's not exactly right. My head fills with the smell of yeast. All of my memories of my grandmother are coated with a mixture of sunlight, dust, and the smell of yeast. I can mold her face in my mind, compassionate, intelligent, bleak. I can trace her high cheek bones, the life lines etched in her skin, the deep caves where her eyes peered out as if they belonged to another person. She was in her nineties when I came into the world. I was a teenager when she left it. But if you passed her apartment house early in the morning and saw her scrubbing the stoop, you'd probably think she was a very old young person or a very young old person.

I used to kneel on the floor next to the red oilcloth-covered table in her kitchen so I could see her timeless, precious hands, both over and under the table. Under the table, those hands rested in a luxurious stillness. Above, they made bread for the Sabbath. Elbow deep in flour, she wove her wisdom into me while braiding the egg-yellow dough.

"People have energy which works in their lives the way this yeast does in the bread. At the very center of their beings it pushes, stretches, demands to expand into the world. If they lock it in, keep it from rising"—her fingers tangled in the dough—"their souls get sick. The energy gets confused, it twists and strangles instead of making new patterns." As she struggled to free her hands, the beautiful braid she had shaped was destroyed. She punched the dough flat again, flipped it and sprinkled it, and me, with flour.

"Then we have to go back to the beginning and start all over again with the kneading and rising."

She was a tiny woman, shrunken as if some of the juice had been sucked out from beneath her skin. But her hands were extremely large, the veins risen to the surface, like they did on the mustard-yellow leaves I had pressed between the pages of my Girl Scout handbook. Her long

white fingers reminded me of tree roots plucked right out of the earth.

I can't recall the sound of her voice. I'm not even sure she spoke to me in English, although I don't recall ever knowing Russian or Yiddish. What comes back is her warm palm resting on my forehead, transfusing a luminous stream of stories directly into my brain. The mysteries of the whole world shone like a distant moon in the sensitivity of her hand.

We sat together on the fire escape of her four-room, third-floor walk-up apartment in Hell's Kitchen, New York, every Sunday. My friends in the suburbs would always talk about going to Sunday school; for the longest time, I imagined that they too were taught on their grandmothers' fire escapes. Back and forth I swung my patent Maryjanes while she sat next to me, earnest and distracted, unmoving as if she was carved. She always wore black dresses, with shiny big buttons down the front and a lace edged collar. Her legs were of equal thickness all the way down to her ankles, swollen and heavy, above black clunky leather shoes that had tiny patterns of holes poked around the laces. Our classroom was the teeming streets beneath us with newspapers swirling in the wind. The people who scrambled below were the subjects. She would point one of those long white fingers at a passer-by and ask me what I saw.

Once she pointed at a fat man who stepped out of a gleaming black Buick wearing a raccoon coat. I said he was rich. My mother taught me early on to make the distinctions that separated people into piles like laundry: colored or white, clean or dirty, Gentile or Jew, rich or poor. My grandmother shook her head slowly and clicked her tongue. "Look with your other eyes. Look into his heart. Do you see there is no light there?" I must have nodded, because she whispered in a dry voice, "He is a very poor man. A young soul perhaps. Now look over there."

She pointed to a small boy wearing a red-striped polo shirt who had no legs and wheeled himself down the street on a makeshift board with roller skate wheels. I had seen him many times before, laughing, whistling, joking with the women who leaned out windows to hang their laundry on the lines that stretched from one building to the next.

"But Grandma, that poor boy has no legs!"

"*Ketzaleh,* try something for me. Slip him over your mind as if he were a sweater you were putting on. Feel what it's like to be him. Feel his heart. Now look at him again, look at that heart. It's pure gold and wide as the sky. He's a rich old soul whose path is to teach all of us about joy!"

Her rootfingers often seemed to point to what was invisible, as if she were painting things that could only be seen in a wide, blurry-eyed way. One Sunday, she drew spirals slowly in the air and called them the Wisdom Trail. "Each of us travels this path, round and round the truth at our core. So we come to the same intersections, the same struggles over and over," she said quietly. Transfixed, I stopped chewing the wad of pink Bazooka, and saw what she spoke of in the air in front of us. The taxi horns disappeared, the thick soot and orange rust, the pizza smells from Esposito's restaurant, and the pigeons flapping on the roof across the street all disappeared as Grandma's words set me in the middle of a prismatic spiral.

"People walk this trail shifting from one foot to the other—first a step of risk to learn something new, then a step of mastery so they can live what they've learned. If they only use their foot of risk, they spend their lives hopping nervously from thing to thing. But if they only use their foot of mastery, they get stuck, mired, stagnant. Sometimes they think they're moving backwards, but they're not. It's just that each pass around, if you've gathered more wisdom, is wider, with less effort and more grace. What's important is that wherever you go on the path, there's no way to escape from yourself, or what you came here to do."

Sometimes she frowned slightly so the grooves between her white eyebrows would get very deep, and she seemed to disappear inside herself, to a place of shadows and secrets. Waves of quiet flowed out of her. I floated on those waves, until she answered whatever question that was rising in me before it could live on my lips. One particular dreary Sunday morning after I had just finished reading *The Diary Of Anne Frank,* she told me how each soul is born with something to give, something to learn, something to experience. She told me I would live in an age where people would confuse magic and mystery; where they would struggle to learn to live from their hearts like the boy in the striped shirt rather than the way the man in the raccoon coat did from his stomach. "When your center of gravity is there," she said, pointing to my solar plexus, "you measure the whole world like a bookkeeper: one for you and one for me; I take out the garbage, you wash the dishes. But when your center is here, in your heart, you give just because it fills you up."

Anthony Salvatore Esposito, whose father owned the restaurant on the corner, loved big rocks and stones. Grandma said it was a legacy from his grandfather, who used to be a mason in Italy. On weekends Tony and the old man would go someplace in New Jersey and move big rocks around, crafting walls and walkways, steps and small bridges. She said his grandfather's legacy would fill the pockets of his soul so he would be able to walk his own wisdom trail. I understood that in some way my future would involve helping people make the shift to living from their hearts. The legacy of stories that were saturated with her loving tradition were the mortar with which I crafted my own bridges and stairways.

One Sunday while she was brushing the dense cloud of her silky white hair, I ran my fingers over the meadow flowers carved into the top of a small camphorwood box that had always fascinated me. She came up silently behind me, placed her brush down next to the matching silver hand mirror my father had given her the year before, and put the box in her palm, opening and closing her hand several times.

She said, "Hands, hearts, and boxes can be opened or closed. They're capable of both, yes?" I nodded and she stretched the box out to me. I took it very carefully and pried the lid open with my thumbnail. Inside was a musty smell and a handful of dirt.

"Where did it come from, Grandma?"

"Home."

I looked around the apartment, but she shook her head and I knew then she meant Russia.

"What's it for?"

She took a pinch of the dirt between her fingers and sifted it back into the box. Her voice got cobwebby as she said, "When I left the old country, I had to leave so much behind, so I took this handful of home with me. When we got off the boat on Ellis Island I put a pinch there beneath my feet to make a friend of the strange ground."

I don't know where she learned all she knew since she never went to school in her small village. When I asked one day, her cheeks got flat as if they had been ironed, and those long fingers traced the white carved woman's face on the shell cameo pin she always wore on the collar of her black dress. Her words were wide, floating. "It is the Sisterhood that passes their wisdom through me as if it were a ribbon carried by an invisible needle. They come to me in my dreams. They'll leave ribbons for you too." I squeezed her hand, kissed her cheek, sweet with tiny golden hairs, and then proceeded to plague her with a mosquito swarm of questions. She said no more and didn't mention the Sisterhood again. But she always began our Sunday mornings by asking me about my dreams.

When I was twelve, my grandmother told me that I would have a son, and that there was a very important tradition I must remember to follow with him when he first began to read. Having a son seemed a ridiculous thing to even think about, but traditions I liked. Traditions were candles, and feathers, and mysterious words and moving hands like flowers in wind. She placed her warm open palm on my forehead, and our minds became like two watercolors bleeding into one another.

"When your son learns to read, the very first time, you must give him some honeycake, something sweet to eat. His mind will tie the two things together from that moment on. Learning and sweetness. Don't forget this!"

I asked her if someone had given her something sweet to eat when she was a young reader. She pressed her lips tight. "I never learned to read. We had no books in my village, and besides I was a girl. Girls were for cooking and cleaning, not for books and learning. That's the way it was in the Old Country. That's why I wanted to leave. That, and the Cossacks and pogroms."

I knew she didn't want to talk about those things. Her first two

children were killed in a pogrom, as well as her brother and mother. I wasn't sure what a pogrom actually was. I just knew it had to do with drunken soldiers and Jewish people being shot for fun late at night, because they were Jewish.

I decided not to ask her any more, but I did want to know if she had given my father honeycake when he had learned to read. Her eyes got all red, as if they were bleeding, and her words got sing-songy, as if she were mourning someone who had died.

"We were too poor then for honey. Your grandfather was working in the sweatshop, and eight children were a lot of mouths to feed. We didn't have money for sweet things, and your father had to drop out of school too soon so he could work and help out. He never learned to read too well. It is the one thing I am ashamed of. That is why it is so important that you teach *your* son to love learning. Then it will be all right about your father. His root will sprout through you and your son, and it will be all right. You and your son will learn to read for me, for your father, for the children in the pogrom, for all of us."

The week before she died, my grandmother came to stay at our house. This was the only time I had ever seen her outside of Hell's Kitchen and I knew she missed what was familiar and comforting to her. She moved as if she were swimming in sawdust, her body a heavy doleful burden she must advance from room to room. She sat collapsed on the olive green couch in the den. My father was so proud of that room, its walls lined with pickled pine. It was one of the first houses in New Rochelle to have a television. She refused to allow it to be turned on. She shook her head once and said, "No, Villie." That's all it took for the huge lion of a man, president of a major corporation, leader of thousands, who strapped me regularly, to hang his head obediently and leave the television untouched.

My lime green parakeet Tippy also lived in the den. He was seven years old, hung upside down in his cage, and pecked silently at his own reflection in a small round mirror. Each of us had tried for years to teach him to speak. Each of us had given up. The day after my grandmother died the telephone rang in the den. We were having tea at the yellow

Formica table in the kitchen. We heard grandma's thickly accented voice say, "Villie, answer the goddamned phone." My father and I rushed together through the louvered doors. The room was empty. He glanced nervously around. Actually, the phone hadn't rung, but he picked up the receiver anyway. The dial tone was loud in the silent echoes of the room. Just as we were returning to the kitchen, the same voice said, "Villie, answer the goddamned phone." The voice had not come from the olive green couch, but from Tippy's cage.

That night, after everyone was asleep, I shuffled into the den, lifted the palm tree printed chintz cover my mother had made for Tippy's cage, and slid the little door up. I stuck my skinny finger in and he hopped on, scratching me with his beak the way he always did. I pulled him out slowly. Tippy scrambled up to my wrist as I opened the back door and walked out under the night sky. My chest rattled with emotion as I looked up. I could feel my grandmother's last story thrumming in my mind as if she still had her palm wide on my forehead: "Everyone has an island in their heart," she said, "but most people forget when they grow up. You know eventually each of us loses everything that's precious to us, at least on the outside. That's just the way life is meant to be. But what is on the island is ours to keep forever. So it's important, very important, to really enjoy what we love, to absorb it so deeply into you that it will take root on the island. Then it belongs to you forever."

Tippy climbed up my outstretched arm and rested on my shoulder. He nibbled my ear lobe and then stretched out his wings, tilting his head from one side to the other. He must have flapped before he took off, but I don't remember that. He seemed to hop onto an invisible long white finger, lifting him into the untamed blackness.

Can you hear her whispering from the island?

"*Ketzaleh*, don't forget to tell them to eat some honeycake after they read these stories. The boys and the girls. The men and the women. The Russians and the Americans. Remind them all to eat some honeycake so their minds will tie the two things together from now on—learning and sweetness. Remember this!"

FOR MY GRANDMOTHERS

Pauline Brunette Danforth

I write for those who cannot speak,
voices unrehearsed.
Grandmothers who came before me whisper silent words—
They are the already born within me
clamoring to be free.
Grandmothers young and old
prod me to tell their stories,
many untold . . .

"My mother she has no warm clothes to wear.
Ten yards of calico, two dresses will do,
give her some shoes and maybe some stockings too."
May-mah-be-quay complains,
"All I do is take care of her. My time is all spent on her—
Toothless, blind, sick all the time, she's nearly lame too."

Pe-wash-bick-oquay sits by the window, fear in her eyes:
"They've taken my son Nin-gwiss far away—
When the maple sap flowed he ran in the woods,
by summer he sat very still.
The Doctor told me it's TB and polio."
At the window she waits patiently to hear of his death.

Wash-we-yay-cumig-oke curses her guards—
They don't understand her words.
"Bigid-ishin Release me!" she shouts,
"Fishing is not a crime, it's our way of life.

My daughter is sick. She needs fish soup.
I must be let go. Your laws are not mine to obey."

Grandmothers, complainers and nags,
they poke at me and tug my sleeve.
"Listen to us, granddaughter,
our voices are real, the stories did happen—
our time has gone by, but our pain lingers on.
Tell our stories, learn from our lives.
Keep our words with you, don't let our ways die."

ROSAURA, MY GRANDMOTHER

Lilly Mary Vigil

Rosaura Lucero Vigil was a woman of quiet strength, who lived in a time and place where hardship was a part of everyday life. She was born in Paraje, New Mexico, during the time of the Civil War. A small village on the east side of the Rio Grande, Paraje was the last outpost before heading south into the waterless Jornada Del Muerto. She finally settled in Lemitar, a small farming community located along the river just north of Socorro. She was tall, large boned and dark skinned due to her mixture of Plains Indian, Pueblo Indian, and Spanish bloods. Rosaura wore traditional clothing consisting of long sleeved dresses, gray print apron and cotton mantas tied around her head. The manta was always silk on Sundays.

My grandmother taught me to believe in miracles. One evening, when my father was a young boy, Rosaura had just finished preparing dinner. She arranged the table with her tin plates and spoons and the family sat down for their meal of potatoes. Suddenly, rocks began to drop from the ceiling! They fell all around the table, though not a single plate or person was touched. When it stopped, the children were asked to take the rocks outside. The village priest came to bless the house, but still the rocks continued to rain for two more weeks. My grandmother's simple acceptance of this and other similar events must have given her hope against the overwhelming hardships she faced. To her they were miracles.

Rosaura was married at fourteen, which was commonplace in the nineteenth century. During her lifetime, she had seventeen children. Her last child, my father, was born when she was forty-eight years old. I was always aware of a deep sadness about her, but only later did I understand that it was because ten of her babies died in infancy. Her father and brother were killed in an Apache raid in the 1880s and the influenza epidemic took her husband and a married daughter in the

early 1920s. She lived a life of hard work, scraping by to feed her family. Never did she complain or show indignation at the poverty or over-whelming responsibility she must have felt. My grandma was an example of tenacity and forbearance, qualities I have been grateful for in my life many times.

As a child I traveled vast distances across the Southwest to visit my grandma. She shared the family stories during those visits. As I listened quietly at her side, she would stroke my cheek or smile at me. She often asked if I could stay and keep her company. I enjoyed these times because I was totally immersed in my culture. We worked in her primitive kitchen, one of three small adobe rooms where she had raised her family. We prepared beans, corn and other foods from her garden. She actually spoke very little, but the air was rich with her presence.

Looking back, the seemingly unexplainable events of the rock shower were taken as a normal spiritual occurrence and required no further explanation. This was the common attitude of the people during this time. Remembering this story gave me strength when I was a young mother. I always wanted to pursue my love of art even while raising four children. I took art classes in the morning and painted late into the night. Rosaura always advised her children to "live a little for yourself." I kept her words alive and reached for what I wanted. Now, involved with the fine arts, I have surrounded myself with my culture, creating the same feeling I had when I was a little girl visiting my grandma. I have what I want and I know who I am. She gave me this.

MEMORIAL DAY

Virginia Haiden

I go to the cemetery to visit my grandmother's grave,
a rusty trowel in my hand to cut away
the sod from the stone that says, "Mother."
I am secretly happy to see that the earth
is swollen and raised, happy to think
that the roots of the elm have opened your casket.
I lean my cheek on the rough bark of the tree,
feel the warmth of the sun,
see your eyes in pale celadon of new leaves.
I sprinkle grass seed on your grave,
rye grass, bent grass, grass for the shade.

For you, there was always the dark call of the dead,
the room swathed in black, the speaking to spirits,
to people long gone. I think of your picture at twenty,
your hair lit behind you like a kerosene lamp,
and the bruised eyes already stunned
with the hand that life was to deal you.
I think that if you had known then what was to come,
you would have swung yourself from some high tree
behind the barn on the Strawberry River.

I remember your green rooms, filled with polished oleander,
    poinsettias tall as trees, dark ferns curving to light,
and violets, violets, in every window, and always,
a singing bird in a silver cage.
From you, I learned planting by the moon,
learned the healing herbs, learned how to listen
to what was said without being spoken.

With your tales of long ago, you taught me that time
was like a river, showed me plates from Prussia,
spoons embossed with flowers from an ancient garden,
and the centuries-old crystal cup carved
with the cameos of a long-forgotten empress.
I touched the quilt your mother made—moved my palm
across the shawl worn on the sailing ship from Germany,
your father's Sunday suit, first days of school.
"These will be your daughter's," you said to me,
"and they will be your daughter's daughter's."
And as mirror reflects in mirror, I saw an infinity
of little girls, all sitting on your lap,
eating peaches from your crystal cup.

Conjure woman, old magician,
I still hold the lifeline you threw me—
both the dark loving for the dead,
and the love for that which is yet to be born. . . .

PERFECT MISERY

Stephanie Patterson

My Grandmother Patterson had two great loves in her life: the Christian Science religion and country and western music. The inherent contradiction in this may not have been obvious to everyone, but I saw it clearly. While as a Christian Science practitioner she was dedicated to the proposition that the world was without sin or illness, she relished the drinking, infidelity and just plain bad luck rampant in country's tortured ballads. The complexities of her character could perhaps best be captured by a collaboration between Stephen King and Tennessee Williams—*Misery on a Hot Tin Roof.*

Oda Patterson was not a big woman, but few people, especially members of her family, realized this when caught in the Venus fly trap of her personality. Her children, who understood the danger if not the attraction, kept their distance. Her oldest son cut all ties when he left high school and moved to New England. He sent yearly Christmas cards with no return address. My father made his exit by joining the Navy and maintaining his own special brand of radio silence. When my grandmother contacted the Red Cross and complained that he never wrote her, a practice which caused her to worry incessantly that the Northern Koreans had captured her boy and were lighting bamboo shoots that they had forced under his fingernails, he wrote a letter which said simply, "Mother, I'm writing this because the Red Cross says I have to. Tom."

My own relationship with my grandmother was singularly complicated. My disability, which seemed a stubborn inability on my part to walk without the aid of braces, was a reproach to the Christian Science ideal of perfection, but it was also a fulfillment of the country and western music ethic. Country music was filled with talk songs in which tortured parents confided to sleeping children their myriad fears about what the future might hold. My grandmother's religious beliefs seemed at war with her love of poster child pathos.

I did not see my grandmother often. She would appear every five years or so without warning. One afternoon as I sat engrossed in a Nancy Drew mystery, I heard a tapping sound. I looked up to find Grandmother Patterson striking a lethal-looking red nail against a window. This visit, like all her others, was disconcerting. She sported a hairdo I had not seen before. Her beehive looked like a confection made of egg whites that had been beaten a few seconds too long. Her makeup was heavy and several shades too dark for her complexion.

"Hello! Hello! Hello!" she shouted in the Texas drawl she affected for her northern campaign. She grabbed my jaw and hit my lips with hers. Though she exchanged awkward pleasantries with my mother, I could feel her watching me as I went to get her a Dr. Pepper.

My grandmother never said a word to me about my disability, but I knew she sent my parents letters in which she reminded them that all God's children are perfect and urged them to tell me of God's perfect love. She dismissed my good grades as a matter of course—signs of that inherent perfection.

When my parents told her I had done particularly well in a public speaking class, she looked shocked: "Well, I bet you're right shy."

I was not the only family member who squirmed under my grandmother's gaze. I knew my father, often aloof and hard to please, was weary of trying to prove that he was a successful adult—a weariness which must have become unbearable as my grandmother countered each of his stories of triumph with some tale of another parent's son who was taking the world by storm.

My father managed to convey his disappointment in himself and his dislike of his mother to me. The feeling that confronting my grandmother would please my father, combined with the fact that I played out my adolescence in the 1960s, made a clash inevitable.

Grandmother Patterson displayed the smug complacency of someone who had never had her prejudices challenged, and I yearned to disabuse her of the notion that I was "right shy." We had our clash

during this particular visit, over the unlikely object of my admiration—Lyndon Baines Johnson.

My LBJ was not the teller of crude tales or the grandiose leader who was to find himself mired in "the big muddy" of Vietnam. My LBJ shepherded the 1964 Civil Rights Act through Congress with more singleness of purpose than Jack Kennedy ever showed. He faced the country and let a lot of scared old white guys know that they would pass the Voting Rights Act "because it's not just Negroes, but really it's all of us who must overcome the crippling legacy of bigotry and injustice. And we *shall* overcome."

My grandmother was an avid Lyndon hater. She was a student of a body of literature that provided rationales for her hatred. Her favorite volumes were *A Texan Looks at Lyndon* and *None Dare Call It Treason*, a book distributed by the John Birch Society. My grandmother quoted these as if they were sacred texts.

Usually when my grandmother went into one of her tirades about Lyndon, I would just sit quietly, but during this visit she was a little shriller and I was feeling bolder. So before she got too far in enumerating the sins in LBJ, I interrupted.

"If you're going to read about Lyndon Johnson, you shouldn't read trash," I said.

My father laughed. My grandmother looked at me as if an inanimate object had spoken.

"Those books are just written by bigoted people who don't like Negroes. They don't like anyone who looks different." I began to go on about this, all the while thinking about the restrictions people imposed on me because of my disability and my frequent exclusion from a teenage social life.

Finally, in exasperation, my grandmother said, "Watch your mouth, young lady. You're startin' to sound like one of those niggers."

"Well, sometimes I feel like one of those niggers."

"You're gettin' uppity enough to be one."

"Thank you," I said.

It was the only compliment my grandmother ever paid me.

PERSONAL EFFECTS

for Mary Margaret Gleason

Mary Scott

Because I was the first grandchild, your namesake,
I inherited your wedding ring set,
tarnished pieces of silver you never used,
and your paint-splattered, battered metal paint box.
Apprehensive as an archaeologist
entering a Pharaoh's tomb, I opened it
expecting a curse, your harsh admonitions.

"Art doesn't pay," you warned me when I confessed
a yearning to be an artist. You learned to paint
when you were sixty. I was ten and wanted
your unconditional love. You were complex,
no Grandma Moses of primitive statements.
I believed art would draw us closer, paint us
into a corner, force us to confront love.

An autopsy of the box disclosed a mass of shriveled tubes,
caps off, crusted with paint scabs: Raw Sienna, Paynes Gray,
Ivory Black, Chrome Yellow, and Cerulean Blue,
the color of your eyes before they faded.
Reed-like tapered brushes, their bristles stiff,
lay heaped in a pile like gnawed, discarded bones.

Did this clutter really belong to
the fastidious grandmother who made me
wash dishes over, criticized the stripes that
ran off-center down the front of a sewn dress?

"Paints are too expensive," you complained.
I used the chalks you gave me when I was eight
until they were nubs; even now I keep them.

A yellowed, rumpled sheet from the *L.A. Times*
reveals a clue, its date just two days before
your seventy-fifth birthday. Was that when you
declared you were too old and packed up the paints?
That spring I took my first oil painting lesson.
Seven years later you died, leaving the paints,
dried beyond use, to me, who never listened.

Now I understand, Grandma, the message in
this medium. You were right; art does not pay.
It demands more than you could afford to give.
I had nothing to lose and staked everything
on getting close to you. At last I touch you,
clasp these brushes as I would your fingers,
caress paper as I would your creased cheek.

BOBE TILLIE KNOWS A GIRL

Helen Michaelson

"Bobe Tillie knows a girl . . . ," my sister, aunt, or mother mimicked with an exasperated laugh. For thus began each of my grandmother's warnings. Anytime a family member decided to do something she deemed remotely dangerous, decided to do anything at all really, Bobe Tillie would reach into her grab bag of experience and pull from it, like a white rabbit in a magician's hat, an unfortunate example, some sweet innocent thing who met with disaster attempting that same activity. You want to go sailing—Bobe Tillie knows a girl who fell in the water and was eaten by sharks. Roller skating—Bobe Tillie knows a girl who broke her leg and had to have it amputated. A shopping trip—Bobe Tillie knows a girl who vanished without a trace on her way to Jacobson's department store.

"I'm going to the beach," I announced, sweeping through the den on my way out the door.

Bobe Tillie, whose job it was to "babysit" that week while my parents were away, sat forward in her chair. "Are you sure that's safe? At this time of day?"

"It's four o'clock!" I shouted, determined to wander the gloomy ocean front alone.

I was fourteen and I loved taking long walks, drawing my initials on the sand next to Luke MacGregor's. Luke, a normal fourteen-year-old boy, was too interested in hockey to know I was alive, but nonetheless I set aside the two-mile walk every afternoon as a special time to dream of him and hopefully lose those five pounds and keep my complexion clear like *Seventeen* magazine recommended so that maybe then I'd be perfect and Luke would notice me.

"I know a girl . . . ," Bobe Tillie began, her finger shaking along with her high, "old ladyish" voice.

"Oh no!"

"Bobe Tillie knows a girl . . . ," my sister laughed, looking up from her book momentarily.

"I'm fine, Bobe!" I insisted, kissed her quickly on the cheek and ran out the door. As I turned the corner at the end of the driveway I could see Bobe standing at the window watching after me. Her oversize glasses made her look like a worried owl.

"Bobe Tillie knows a girl . . . ," I muttered to myself. I'd barely had a minute alone all week. It felt like we were babysitting my grandmother rather than the other way around. We came right home after school. We kept her company in the living room all evening, rather than escaping to our rooms. Really, my sister and I were old enough to stay by ourselves. "As soon as Carol gets her driver's license," I reasoned, enjoying the freshness of the wind on my face, "we won't need Bobe to stay with us anymore."

I reached the ocean front and climbed through the row of brambles onto the beach. The water was a beautiful moody shade of grey, waves churning furiously on its surface. I plucked a stick off the ground and started to write. "L.M. + H . . ." I left off. Bobe's expression, her sad look at the window haunted me. I shouldn't have been so short with her. But why did she have to be so nervous about everything? If something bad was going to happen, it would happen. You couldn't stay home all day, locked in the house, thinking that would protect you from harm.

I walked on, dragging the stick behind me, tracing a line in the wet sand. When I reached the breakwater, a pile of gigantic boulders fifty yards down the beach, I stopped. There I perched on my favorite rock, and gazed out to sea. I tried to think of Luke . . . how he'd stop by my locker one day, hook his arm casually over the top of its open door, his blue eyes sparkling . . . But again, all I could see was my grandmother, her brown eyes wide with worry.

I jumped off the rock. I could make it back home in just fifteen minutes. I'd kiss her hello, show her I was fine. "See it's perfectly safe to walk around here," I'd say.

I turned toward the road, and there, standing quietly watching over

me, was Bobe! She had followed me! The blood pounded in my ears. How could she! She'd spied!

"Getting some exercise?" I asked angrily, stepping over a log back onto the pavement.

Bobe shrugged apologetically, "Well, you know..." Her brows were knit closely together and she was breathing heavily. It must have been quite a walk for her. My anger melted away, replaced by guilt. My own grandmother was afraid of me.

I reached out and took Bobe's hand. The skin hung loosely around her knuckles; it felt strangely soft and rough at the same time. Bobe looked anxiously up the road toward home, gearing herself up for the long walk ahead.

"Isn't it pretty down here?" I asked. Bobe turned to face the water. A red and black barge chugged through the waves, sea gulls circling above it. Bobe's hand tightened around mine. "Yes, I can see why you like it here."

I smiled and squeezed her hand. Then we headed towards home together, walking slowly.

THE GOOD STUFF

Learning About Life from Grandma Val

Louise Freeman-Toole

As a child, I lived vicariously through my grandmother. She lived on a tiny island in the vast Alaskan wilderness, while I lived in a California beach town. I had never met my grandmother, and she loomed in my imagination as a larger-than-life personality, a storybook figure I could claim as my own. She was a Robinson Crusoe with her man Friday, living a self-sufficient life far from civilization; she was Dr. Doolittle calling deer to eat from her hand; she was a pioneer woman melting snow for drinking water and cooking venison on a wood stove.

When I finally met my Grandma Val, I was eleven years old and she was everything the wood smoke that clung to her letters had promised. With her straight grey hair cut short like a man's, her fingers stained with nicotine, she was nothing like a grandmother was supposed to be: she was not powdered, coiffed and soft; she smoked, drank, swore, wore pants, and told funny stories. I was utterly enthralled. To my lasting regret, it was the only time I ever saw her.

Ten years later I flew to Sitka, Alaska, to attend Val's funeral. In her basement I found several boxes of journals from the island years. At last, I thought, I'll get to hear the whole story, not just the tantalizing glimpses I'd had as a child. I took the journals home and stayed up many nights reading them. But I was surprised and disappointed by their lack of drama. Where was the danger and excitement I remembered hearing about? Instead, the daily entries detailed the courtship of ducks in the bay, the glitter of frost on fir needles, the garden that thrived in the long days of summer. I realized that when a bear prowled around the cabin or a search-and-rescue mission for a downed plane was being organized, she had no time to write. It was on the quiet days with no visitors, when fog and rain shrouded the little island, that she had time to write.

Then I ran across a journal kept by Val's husband, Scotty. An old Alaska sourdough with many tales of past encounters with sinking

boats, wolves, dynamite and other dangers, Scotty considered their life quite unremarkable. His entries for a typical week on the island: Christmas Day—Just another day. Dec. 26—Nothing much. Dec. 27—More of the same. Dec. 28—Ho hum. Dec. 29—Just this and that.

I had to laugh at this dour Scot's view of their life, but I was grateful for it as well, because I realized that, like Scotty, I'd been looking for the "good stuff," dismissing their daily routine as "nothing much."

I went back to my grandmother's journals, telling myself to slow down. I came to appreciate Val's perceptive eye trained by years of newspaper work. In her neat handwriting, the island came alive for me. I could hear the otter eating a fish, "chomping with his mouth open wide and happy"; the deer calling her fawns with a "half-musical, half-guttural sound, faintly reminiscent of a gull's cry far away"; the Canadian geese that "synchronize the beat of their wings like cylinders alternating in a smooth-running gasoline engine"; the killer whale heard late one night from the porch, exhaling "the biggest eeriest sigh imaginable, primordial, monstrous."

Gradually, I fell into the rhythm of their days. I started to hear the ever present "slap, slurp and rattle of the tide among the little loose flat rocks of the beach." I ducked as an accumulation of snow slid off the roof like "a load of coal going down a chute." I saw winter ice "piled like old fashioned soap flakes on the beach," and the summer "strawberries blooming extravagantly like stars dropped in the tall grass." I breathed "the mingled smells of forest spice, salt tang, and whiffs of cedar wood smoke."

I saw, in the careful attention she paid to everything around her, my grandmother's struggle to understand and adapt to this new environment, so different from her former home in southern California. I thought of Joseph Campbell's words: "Move into a landscape. Find the sanctity of that land. And then there can be the matching of your own nature with this gorgeous nature of the land." Val had done exactly that: she had watched and listened and absorbed all she could. Learning new skills and overcoming old fears, she had found a place for herself.

I had enjoyed lingering in the pages of Val's journals, but when I

closed the last notebook and found myself again in my split-level house, far from Alaska, with the sound of my children playing in the yard and the neighbor's lawn mower buzzing, I felt no discontinuity between my grandmother's life and my own. Life did not have to be a thrill a minute, I realized. In her celebration of the simple, the everyday, the beautiful, Val had shown me the *real* good stuff; by showing me how she lived her life, my grandmother had shown me how to live my own life. Pay attention, I learned, to small things around you; be thankful; immerse yourself in your surroundings; accept that some days will glide by like water, and other days will fight back like an unwieldy chunk of wood that resists being fed to the fire; don't limit yourself by sticking to what you already know; keep striving; look forward to old age, for it brings satisfactions of its own. And above all: keep your eyes open and your pen ready.

THE GRANDMOTHER SONGS

Linda Hogan

The grandmothers were my tribal gods.
They were there
when I was born. Their songs
rose out of wet labor
and the woman smell of birth.

From a floating sleep
they made a shape around me,
a grandmother's embrace,
the shawl of family blood
that was their song for kinship.

There was a divining song
for finding the lost,
and a raining song
for the furrow and its seed,
one for the hoe
and the house it leaned against.

In those days, through song,
a woman could fly
to the mother of water
and fill her ladle
with cool springs of earth.

She could fly to the deer
and sing him down to the ground.

Song was the pathway where people met
and animals crossed.

Once, flying out of the false death of surgery,
I heard a grandmother singing for help.
She came close
as if down a road of screaming.

It was the terror grandmother.
I'd heard of her.
And when our fingers and voices met,
the song
of an older history came through
my mouth.

At death, they say
everything inside us opens,
mouth, heart, even the ear opens
and breath passes
through the memories
of loves and faces.
The embrace opens
and grandmothers pass,
wearing sunlight
and thin rain,
walking out of fire
as flame
and smoke
leaving the ashes.

That's when rain begins,
and when the mouth of the river sings,
water flows from it
back to the cellular sea
and along the way
earth sprouts and blooms, the grandmothers
keep following the creation
that opens before them
as they sing.

"Dying is a wild night and a new road."
Emily Dickenson

Occasionally, if one is fortunate, a precious gift may arise from the experience of loss. This happens especially when true attention is given to the passage, when meaning is assigned to the transaction between loved ones. The passing of a grandmother involves the transmission of lineage and legacy. For a granddaughter, this burden of love requires adequate grieving, assimilation, and courage to hold forth with the gifts gained. We expect death to be shattering (often it is) and final, but for many granddaughters death was also a window through which lessons and loving (and even humor) continue to illuminate.

BIRTHDAY POEM FOR MY GRANDMOTHER

(for L. B. M. C., 1890–1975)

Sharon Olds

I stood on the porch tonight—which way do we
face to talk to the dead? I thought of the
new rose, and went out over the
grey lawn—things really
have no color at night. I descended
the stone steps, as if to the place where one
speaks to the dead. The rose stood
half-uncurled, glowing white in the
black air. Later I remembered
your birthday. You would have been ninety and getting
roses from me. Are the dead there
if we do not speak to them? When I came to see you
you were always sitting quietly in the chair,
not knitting, because of the arthritis,
not reading, because of the blindness,
just sitting. I never knew how you
did it or what you were thinking. Now I
sometimes sit on the porch, waiting,
trying to feel you there like the colors of the
flowers in the dark.

THE END OF THE REIGN OF QUEEN HELEN (1894–1985)

Christina Gombar

I remember first the mouth. Always open, mauve tongue cracked down the center from seven decades of use, disappearing into cavernous blackness beyond. Granny Gombar had a voice like a bull horn, ruined she said, from swallowing a fish bone at twenty-five. I suspected the Salems. I see one smoldering, caught in the bird's beak of a silver sculptured ashtray. I see her, through a haze of years and smoke, smoke and sun, slatting through blinds from the treeless yard. The affronted black eyes behind the butterfly glasses, the yellow skin, flat nose, white, tightly curled hair: the girth loosely encased in a flowered shift, the wide feet in cloth wedge sandals, and the wide mouth—always open.

"My son the doctor," she bragged to her neighbors about my father who, in fact, was only a dentist.

That voice, screaming repartee at her powder blue parakeet Bootsie (1962–1965). "You're late!" she'd bellow into the phone to my parents who used to drop my sister and me at her apartment for a few terrifying hours every few weeks. There, by the tea table, under the embroidered portrait of three cats in dresses jumping into a lily-pad pond, among the white ceramic figurines of shepherdesses and swans in eighteenth-century dress, Granny reigned.

She bought us coloring books, but wouldn't let us color. We sat idly by, watching her neatly fill in Bambi, Cinderella, or Lady and the Tramp. She never let us go near Bootsie. I wanted to take him/her/it, touch its pale blue feathers and squeeze it so its little purpley-black tongue would pop out. Bootsie was the last in line of her revered pets, the most notorious of which was a canine called Mitzi (1938–1947) who was fed scrap meat from a restaurant. "That dog ate better than we did," my father recalls bitterly.

"Eat! Eat! Eat!" she'd bellow at me. I was frozen with terror.

"You're not a Gombar!" she would shout at six-year-old me. "You're like your mother's family. You've got those round cat eyes."

"I was a beauty," she would sometimes proclaim. Impossible to tell. Few photographs were taken in that family, as if there was nothing to celebrate. The earliest traceable picture of her is at sixty, her looks already obscured by glasses and garish fashions. The occasion: my father's college graduation (first in the family), where he stands pompadoured, but otherwise like a prisoner between his dour father and gloating mother.

"This is the year," she would proclaim. "I had a dream." Hand over heart, upper arms billowing, bulk settled into the big easy chair. "For my funeral I want a high mass and I want her (pointing to my older sister) to sing 'Ave Maria.'" Rosemary had the voice.

"She'll never die," her sons would declare.

"Work! Work! Work!" was Granny's battle cry. Imminent financial disaster was predicted if my father took a day off with the flu, or two weeks off for a summer vacation.

"You're killing him," she told my mother, after she produced a fourth child—a boy finally—too late in life.

I was told that Granny:

Had secretly dressed Uncle Russell as a girl.

Drove her husband to an early grave.

Drove Mitzi to an early grave.

Drove Bootsie to an early grave.

"I told the doctor—don't tell me I'm frigid! I had three children!"

As a teenager, I began to understand her.

"I wanted to be a nurse!" she told us. "I went through all the training, and then my father said 'I don't want you looking at naked men!'" To escape her father she married Mike at nineteen.

But Mike stayed out nights and without warning escaped to the navy, a four-year hitch. Helen moved back to her father's in shame and disgrace. And then, "I was in the kitchen rolling out the dough for a strudel, when I looked up and saw him standing there in the doorway.

I thought he was a ghost. I went up and hit him with the rolling pin." Their first appearance as a reunited couple was at the doctor's office, to repair Mike's broken collar bone.

"I didn't know where babies came from," she said innocently in her baritone. "On my wedding night I thought Mike was trying to kill me."

"I always wanted a girl," Granny confessed. "When I got pregnant a second time I was sure it was going to be a girl. I made all the little dresses"—pantomiming sewing—"I bought a doll. I was going to call her"—eyes closed behind the butterfly glasses— "*Gloria*."

But Gloria turned out to be Uncle Russell, who took the fanatical neatness and excitability that were Granny's own trademarks to extremes, joined the marines at the start of World War II, got tattooed, kept his buzz cut to the end of his days, collected guns.

"*You* tell them," she said, meaning our boyfriends, "if they don't treat my girls right, I'll go after them with my cane!" She brandished her weapon only in her imagination—now she used a walker.

When I was nineteen, Granny suffered a heart attack and stayed with us to recuperate. "What's wrong with him," she fretted primly in her bullhorn voice about her-son-the-doctor, "that he won't eat what your mother cooks and makes a mess on the stove at midnight?"

Between this disorderly atmosphere and the lack of Salems, it was all in all a disquieting stretch, and soon she was back in her apartment, with Salem Lights and an oxygen tank for when the emphysema kicked in.

"I'm glad to see one of my girls get married before I kick the bucket." At Rosemary's reception she sat on a fold-out chair, like a great jewelled frog in green satin, bearing an affronted look. The fact was, my sister's husband and Granny had taken one look at each other, resulting in instant and mutual disgust. "You tell him—my cane," Granny said, pulling my sister's arm at one point.

I was home alone at my parents' house one sunny Sunday when the call came. My Uncle Russell, who should have been a girl, walked into Granny's apartment in his crew-cut and tattoos after the six o'clock mass. In the bedroom: curtains floating and sun streaming in, the walker knocked over, Granny splayed, facedown on the bed.

"Your grandmother's dead," Russell told me over the phone in his bullhorn voice, copied, like so much else, from her. From his tone, you would have thought it was something he'd done.

Russell took charge of the funeral, and with his mania for efficiency and detail arranged for everything so swiftly that there was no time to ponder, no time to come up with the right words, and no one to sing "Ave Maria."

I knelt at the casket to pray, trying to imagine Granny in the afterlife. I only came up with a vision of her shrouded in cigarette smoke, a host of pale parakeets swirling about her white head.

I looked down. She made a marvelous corpse. She had scarcely lost any bulk in her last years, despite finally succumbing to dentures. She was dusted white, well-rouged, and arrayed in the same jewel-green dress she'd worn to my sister's wedding. (She still resembled a dressed-up frog.) On her mouth, the same deep red lipstick. Something different about her mouth, though. What? Then I realized—it was the first time I'd ever seen it shut.

RECIPE FOR GRIEF

Barbara Crooker

My grandmother is dying in the hospital.
I cannot comprehend these words,
cannot feel grief, not yet.
Instead, I slice eggplant in a sunny kitchen,
dust it, pat each slice gently.
The flour is as fine and white as her skin.
I enter the ritual:
from flour to eggs to crumbs to oil,
moving in a pattern old as Sicily.
Working against burns and spills,
I assemble the golden slices,
alike as a party of aunts,
tomato sauce fragrant
with basil, oregano,
creamy mozzarella,
pungent parmesan.
In the heat of the oven,
they will meld
into something unlike the sum of their parts.
I've heard her voice in every direction,
her hands are working in mine,
as we create sun drenched Italy, ancient hills of thyme.
Fragrance steams from the oven, as the heady flavors mingle:
this parmigiana, this sacrament, this easing of the heart.

BODILY HARM

Margaret Atwood

[The story of Rennie's mastectomy, the consequent breakup of her relationship with Jake, and a hair-raising deliverance from hopelessness on a Caribbean island is told in a series of flashbacks. Rennie's grandmother's unwinding serves as a beacon throughout her ordeal.]

One of the first things I can remember, says Rennie, is standing in my grandmother's bedroom. The light is coming through the window, weak yellowish winter light, everything is very clean, and I'm cold. I know I've done something wrong, but I can't remember what. I'm crying. I'm holding my grandmother around both legs, but I didn't think of them as legs, I thought of her as one solid piece from the neck down to the bottom of her skirt. I feel as if I'm holding on to the edge of something, safety, if I let go I'll fall, I want forgiveness, but she's prying my hands away finger by finger. She's smiling; she was proud of the fact that she never lost her temper.

I know I will be shut in the cellar by myself. I'm afraid of that, I know what's down there, a single light bulb which at least they leave on, a cement floor which is always cold, cobwebs, the winter coats hanging on hooks beside the wooden stairs, the furnace. It's the only place in the house that isn't clean. When I was shut in the cellar I always sat on the top stair. Sometimes there were things down there, I could hear them moving around, small things that might get on you and run up your legs. I, crying because I'm afraid, can't stop, and even if I hadn't done anything wrong I'd still be put down there, for making noise, for crying.

Laugh and the world laughs with you, said my grandmother. *Cry and you cry alone.* For a long time I hated the smell of damp mittens.

I grew up surrounded by old people: my grandfather and my grandmother, and my great-aunts and great-uncles, who came to visit

after church. I thought of my mother as old too. She wasn't, but being around them all the time made her seem old. On the street she walked slowly so they could keep up with her, she raised her voice the way they did, she was anxious about details. She wore clothes like theirs too, dark dresses with high collars and small innocuous patterns, dots or sprigs of flowers.

As a child I learned three things well: how to be quiet, what not to say, and how to look at things without touching them. When I think of that house I think of objects and silences. The silences were almost visible; I pictured them as gray, hanging in the air like smoke. I learned to listen for what wasn't being said, because it was usually more important than what was. My grandmother was the best at silences. According to her, it was bad manners to ask direct questions.

The objects in the house were another form of silence. Clocks, vases, end tables, cabinets, figurines, cruet sets, cranberry glasses, china plates. They were considered important because they had once belonged to someone else. They were both overpowering and frail: overpowering because threatening. What they threatened you with was their frailty; they were always on the verge of breaking. These objects had to be cleaned and polished once a week, by my grandmother when she was still well enough and afterward by my mother. It was understood that you could never sell these objects or give them away. The only way you could ever get rid of them was to will them to someone else and then die.

The objects weren't beautiful, most of them. They weren't supposed to be. They were only supposed to be of the right kind: the standard aimed at was not beauty but decency. That was the word, too, among my mother and my aunts, when they came to visit. "Are you decent?" they would call gaily to one another before opening the bedroom or bathroom doors. Decency was having your clothes on, in every way possible.

If you were a girl it was a lot safer to be decent than to be beautiful. If you were a boy, the question didn't arise; the choice was whether or not you were a fool. Clothes could be decent or indecent. Mine were always decent, and they smelled decent too, a wool smell, mothballs and a hint of furniture polish. Other girls, from families considered shoddy and loose, wore questionable clothes and smelled like violets. The opposite of decent wasn't beautiful, but flashy or cheap. Flashy, cheap people drank and smoked, and who knew what else? Everyone knew. In Griswold, everyone knew everything sooner or later.

So you had your choice, you could decide whether people would respect you or not. It was harder if your family wasn't respectable but it could be done. If your family wasn't respectable, though, you could choose not to disgrace it. The best way to keep from disgracing it was to do nothing unusual.

The respectability of my family came from my grandfather, who had once been the doctor. Not a doctor, the doctor: they had territories then, like tomcats. In the stories my grandmother told me about him, he drove a cutter and team through blizzards to tear babies out through holes he cut in women's stomachs and then sewed up again, he amputated a man's leg with an ordinary saw, knocking the man out with his fist because no one could hold him down and there wasn't enough whiskey, he risked his life by walking into a farmhouse where a man had gone crazy and was holding a shotgun on him the whole time, he'd blown the head off one of his children and was threatening to blow the heads off the other ones too. My grandmother blamed the wife, who had run away months before. My grandfather saved the lives of the remaining children, who were then put in an orphanage. No one wanted to adopt children who had such a crazy father and mother: everyone knew such things ran in the blood. The man was sent to what they called the loony bin. When they were being formal they called it an institution.

My grandmother worshipped my grandfather, or so everyone said. When I was little I thought of him as a hero, and I guess he was, he was about the closest you could get in Griswold unless you'd been in the war. I wanted to be like him, but after a few years at school I forgot about that. Men were doctors, women were nurses; men were heroes, and what were women? Women rolled the bandages and that was about all anyone ever said about that.

The stories my mother and aunts told about my grandfather were different, though they never told these stories when my grandmother

was there. They were mostly about his violent temper. When they were girls, whenever they skirted what he felt to be the edges of decency, he would threaten to horsewhip them, though he never did. He thought he was lenient because he didn't make his children sit on a bench all Sunday as his own father had. I found it very difficult to connect these stories, or my grandmother's either, with the frail old man who could not be disturbed during his afternoon nap and who had to be protected like the clocks and figurines. My mother and my grandmother tended him the same way they tended me, efficiently and with a lot of attention to dirt; only more cheerfully. Perhaps they really were cheerful. Perhaps it made them cheerful to have him under their control at last. They cried a lot at his funeral.

My grandmother had been an amazing woman of her age; everyone told me that. But after my grandfather's death she began to deteriorate. That's how my mother would put it when her sisters would come to visit. They were both married, which was how they'd got away from Griswold. I was in high school by then so I didn't spend as much time hanging around the kitchen as I used to, but one day I walked in on them and all three of them were laughing, stifled breathless laughs, as if they were being sacrilegious and they didn't want my grandmother to hear them. They hardly saw me, they were so intent on their laughter.

She wouldn't give me a key to the house, my mother said. Thought I'd lose it. This started them off again. Last week she finally let me have one, and I dropped it down the hot air register. They patted their eyes, exhausted as if they'd been running.

Foolishness, said my aunt from Winnipeg. This was my grandmother's word for anything she didn't approve of. I'd never seen my mother laugh like that before.

Don't mind us, my aunt said to me.

You laugh or you cry, said my other aunt.

You laugh or you go bats, said my mother, injecting a little guilt, as she always did. This sobered them up. They knew that her life, her absence of a life, was permitting them their own.

After that my grandmother began to lose her sense of balance. She

would climb up on chairs and stools to get things down, things that were too heavy for her, and then she would fall. She usually did this when my mother was out, and my mother would return to find her sprawled on the floor, surrounded by broken china.

Then her memory began to go. She would wander around the house at night, opening and shutting doors, trying to find her way back to her room. Sometimes she wouldn't remember who she was or who we were. Once she frightened me badly by coming into the kitchen, in broad daylight, as I was making myself a peanut butter sandwich after school. My hands, she said. I've left them somewhere and now I can't find them. She was holding her hands in the air helplessly, as if she couldn't move them.

They're right there, I said. On the ends of your arms.

No, no, she said impatiently. Not those, those are no good anymore. My other hands, the ones I had before, the ones I touch things with.

My aunts kept watch on her through the kitchen window while she wandered around in the yard, prowling through the frost-bitten ruins of the garden which my mother didn't have time to keep up anymore. Once it had been filled with flowers, zinnias and scarlet runner beans on poles where the hummingbirds would come. My grandmother once told me heaven would be like that: if you were good enough you would get everlasting life and go to a place where there were always flowers. I think she really believed it. My mother and my aunts didn't believe it, though my mother went to church and when my aunts visited they all sang hymns in the kitchen after supper when they were doing the dishes.

She seems to think it's still there, said my aunt from Winnipeg. Look. She'll freeze to death out there.

Put her in a home, said my other aunt, looking at my mother's caved face, the mauve half-moons under her eyes.

I can't, my mother would say. On some days she's perfectly all right. It would be like killing her.

If I ever get like that, take me out to a field and shoot me, said my other aunt.

All I could think of at that time was how to get away from Griswold. I didn't want to be trapped, like my mother. Although I admired her— everyone was always telling me how admirable she was, she was practically a saint—I didn't want to be like her in any way. I didn't want to have a family or be anyone's mother, ever; I had none of those ambitions. I didn't want to own any objects or inherit any. I didn't want to cope. I didn't want to deteriorate. I used to pray that I wouldn't live long enough to get like my grandmother, and now I guess I won't.

THE BUCK

Susanna Rich

When I was ten,
Grandmother told me
to get her stuffed when she died
like the buck head by the door
catching webs of evil
in his antlers.

She was to be seated
in the living room
on the sofa
(or chair, our choice),
facing the piano where I would play
Brahms, Liszt and Chopin.

Her eyes were to be open
(maybe a little touch of glass,
for sparkle) and looking upwards
(slightly to the right)
like St. Theresa
or Sebastian pierced with arrows,

her hands—demurely covered
in white lace fingerless gloves—
propped holding the dome of heaven.
Her lips would be slightly open to show
silently parted pearlized teeth,
our guardian angel, mouth of God.

When we went shopping for perfume,
or oil to treat her skin,
or maybe a new pair of gloves
or a light bulb for her ever-burning lamp
she and the buck would wait for our return.

Four times the ten I was,
I still bang a keyboard all day;
dust floats up into my eyes, ears,
mouth, my nose and many pores—
shadow fingers reach
like antlers across my page.
She listens: I sing.

FROGGY GREMLIN,
MY GRANDMOTHER,
AND ME

Joanna Pashdag

I don't remember my grandmother ever being anything but old. My mother was the youngest of ten children, and by the time I was born, her mother was already seventy-four.

We lived in her house in northeast Philadelphia, with thirty-year-old stucco disguising termite-ridden wood walls that were nearly five times as old. We had a front porch with a wicker rocking chair and a rusty metal glider; a living room with a player piano, two Staffordshire dogs, and a brand-new black-and-white television; a dining room just large enough for an old pine trestle table and six well-worn ladderback chairs; and a small, smoky kitchen with cold water and a coal stove.

Upstairs, the front bedroom belonged to my mother and me. Next came my grandparents' room, at least until my grandfather died and my grandmother took ill and moved downstairs to a hospital bed in the living room. At the rear of the upstairs was the house's one bathroom, with a radiator on which my mother would heat water for baths. Looking out the bathroom window, I could look down on our backyard, an overgrown quarter-acre of lilies-of-the-valley, hollyhocks, and weeds.

Because my mother worked, my grandmother took care of me most days after school. When I was learning my ABCs, she bought me a Froggy Gremlin squeaky toy, squeezing it furiously to make an angry ruckus when I got a letter wrong. When I was learning to play the piano, she sat next to me on the bench, singing along to help me keep the melody, even if it was only "Chopstix."

One year, when television westerns and cowboy hats were all the rage, I developed a crush on Dale Starr, a beautiful, blonde "cowgirl"

who hosted a local children's TV show. It was my grandmother who made my costume—a red hat, vest and circle skirt laced with white plastic cord—when I decided I had to be Dale Starr for Halloween. Another year, after we saw *Pinocchio* together, I decided I had to be the Blue Fairy Princess, and while my mother turned one of her old nightgowns into my costume dress, it was my grandmother who made my wings.

Later, as I grew older, she taught me how to make a meatloaf and how to bake a cherry pie; how to hook a rug and how to make a patchwork quilt from old scraps of clothes; and in her infrequent stories of what it was like to marry and bear ten children and watch most of them die, she taught me to survive.

When I was ten, I asked my mother for a rabbit for Easter. She bought me one—a soft, round, furry grey baby doe—along with a baby duckling and a pair of fuzzy yellow chicks. I remember being surprised by how quickly they all grew big, by the fact that the rabbit loved leftover watermelon, and by the fact that once, when I stepped on his paw by accident, the rabbit screamed.

A few months later, when the chicks had grown up into raucous, ugly white hens and my grandmother was out back feeding them—a job that was supposed to be mine—she slipped on a piece of the rabbit's watermelon rind and broke her hip. That was when she moved downstairs into the living room. It was the day after my grandfather had died.

Although her hip never healed, she wasn't entirely bedridden; most days I'd come home from school and find her on the front porch, watching the traffic go by and softly singing "He Walks With Me and He Talks With Me," or another Methodist hymn. I'd sit with her a while, swinging back and forth lazily on the glider. We'd talk then—mostly about what I'd learned that day in school, or what boy in my class I liked, or what boys liked me. But once in a great while, and only after serious prodding and pleading, she'd talk about herself.

The stories would come in tiny bits and pieces, as though the pages in her private diary had become crumpled and faded with time so that only the most indelible memories still remained.

She told me of her Scots-Irish ancestors, including her own grand-mother, Elizabeth Rosebar, who had been the driving force behind her family's migration from the already troubled Derry to the new world.

She told me of the way she felt when she first met the man who was to become my grandfather, James Horrocks. The second son of the second son of a titled Englishman, the rules of primogeniture had left him without an inheritance, but not, she said, without the strength of a line of kings in his eyes. She married a weaver, she said, but in her life he was a true prince until the day he died.

She also told me stories of my mother as a little girl. Words like "fragile," "shy," and "sensitive" told me what I already knew, but told me, too, that my mother had been herself for a very long time. Whatever effects my youthful recklessness and carelessness had had on my mother, I had not been the cause of her turning inward against the world. I was able to sleep a little easier at night because of that.

One day when I came home from school, I found my grandmother still in her bed, not moving, a newspaper lying across her face. I knew she was dead. Frightened half to death myself, I softly stepped closer to her, removed the newspaper and whispered, "Grandmom?" hoping to somehow make her breathe again. Startled, she awoke in fright, eyes wide as dinner plates. Just as startled, I jumped back against the piano, knocking over one of the Staffordshire dogs. The next day, she had replaced the porcelain with my old Froggy Gremlin squeaky toy.

I have a medallion my grandmother gave to my mother when she was a little girl, and which my mother in turn gave to me. On one side is St. Michael, his lance buried deep into a dragon's neck; on the other is a guardian angel. I don't go out without it, or if I do, I am constantly aware of its absence and feel awkward, as if I had gone out in only my underwear. It is not just a family heirloom, and much more than a pretty charm; because it was hers, it is, to me, a talisman, a vital reminder of my real guardian angel, the one who played with me and sang with me, the one who taught me strength, the one who helped me be both a cowgirl and an angel and who taught me that neither one was wrong.

LETTER TO GRANDMA

Kiran A. Thakare

Leaving you
There
in the jaw of cruel *niyati*
thousands of miles away
I came here
to strengthen
my beliefs and
to return
to fight
your war
my war
at home.

Now
three years have passed
you wrote me
"I am anxious to see you
come home soon."
I lied to you,
saying
"*Aattya* I can't come home now
I have some last moments' work to do."
I hide from you
Yes Aattya!
I am trying to make some money
to buy you a gift.

The thought of my return
rejoices me
how proud you will be
to see me
as a grown woman
so strong
so changed
and yet to see
your same naughty GrandDee
as I used to be.

I imagine
on my return
you so happy—
like that *bakuli* plant—
as your GrandDee
is back in your warm nest
and
you telling me
stories of
your lonely monsoons
that you spend
counting
one after another.

I can't wait
to come home
to dance around you
as the *koeil* on the
backyard tree will sing,
to chase your cats from room to room
and follow you in the kitchen

holding the *palloo* of your *sari*
begging for tea
and waiting for that *Dhudh-malai*
Aattya . . .
now I can't wait.

I am ready
with words and swords
to fight our war
a war of
single women
battered women
suppressed women
Reminds me of
Mahabharata
the war
for the right!
for the truth!
and of your sacrifices—
time has come
for the change
and I am ready Aattya
I am ready for the change.

I wrote you
"I will be home
on my birthday twenty-second of February,
twenty more days
and I will be home."
But this time you did not reply.
Why is that Aattya?

perhaps
you are very busy
ordering servants
decorating home and streets
putting "welcome" signs everywhere
planning parties
running here and there
Aattya
I can't wait anymore
my heart sings your songs
as I pack my bags
four more days
sleep well Aattya

18th February, 1993

❧

Today, 20th February,
I received a letter
from your distant relative
he wrote,
"Aattya died last month."

Aattya
I have no words
I am homeless

MIMI, PASSING

Kathlyn Whitsitt Egbert

"I'm eighty-eight years old," Mimi said when they told her about the cancer. "My God, you have to die of something." And then she held the light for us at her own brave vigil. Like all grandmothers, well past the three score and ten the Lord promised, she had to leave. It was time. With old-fashioned decorum we say she has "passed away." People who didn't know her sympathize lightly: "such a long, full life" and so on. Not able to guess what she still meant to us.

"I just hate old women," Mimi herself would often say when her step was slow or eyes dim. Then laugh and go on. Now we know how true it is that "you don't know what you've got until it's gone." Mimi, we didn't have any idea how badly we needed to "help" you. We are not safe as we were. We may never be as loved.

The passing itself was hard. "Help me," she cried out near the end. "Somebody please help me!" And we stroked her, soothed her away from the edge. Her body, harboring its deadly illness for so long, panicked at the last tug and snap as the spirit pulled away. Tumors, Bowels, Liver. The tongue rolls around the words like they are kin, related through their oily consonance. In spite of the ambivalent struggle at the end, I'll bet her spirit was only too glad to be free of her flesh.

"I just want to wake up dead," she used to say. With a true sanguine's low esteem of suffering, she sincerely hoped to avoid the whole scene— especially needles and nursing homes. And, of course, she didn't want to burden her family. By Christmas it became apparent that she was weakening; unseen enemy was on the march. As she dozed in her chair, one evening while her children, grandchildren, and great grand-children moved in the swirl of indoor diversions, a large tower of wooden blocks crashed loudly to the tabletop nearby and startled her awake. She held her hand over her heart, eyes bulging to try to make out what the disaster had been. We all rushed to her side.

"Are you all right, Mimi?"

"Every night I ask God to give me a heart attack," she answered deadpan. Then grinned her famous puckered grin. "You all nearly gave me my wish."

We prayed that God would be so gracious. During the long hard three months it took, we doubted Him, wondered why His mercy lagged behind her need. We had to trust that both He and she would choose the best time. We hunkered down to the daily business of dying. Pain, putrid gases from deep inside the rotting bowels, then crushing weakness and dizziness. Finally, she was forced to the rented hospital bed that she had edged around like a snake. Not so bad, she found. It stayed in the middle of the living room where she wouldn't miss any of the action. She kept her hearing aid in until the day she died and wouldn't turn over on that side to sleep. To the end she hungered after the details of our lives like they were treasure.

The phone rang constantly. I had always said she was my best friend. After she was gone, her closets and drawers yielded dozens of cards, letters, and photos sent to her by people who felt the same about her. A neat trick that. How could so many feel so loved and accepted in such a personal way—the best—all the while knowing perfectly well they were one of many? How did she do it? How does God do it?

There are many big memories that we all share. Mimi loved Russell Stover's candy and was never without a box tucked away somewhere; when her eyes got bad we had to tell her it had tiny ants. She was famous to the kids because she dared to eat cookies and chips all day long and hated vegetables. She also used "bad words" if they served her purpose. Her favorite reading material was the *National Enquirer*; every word she swore was true. Still, she hid it under the sofa cushions when the preacher came. She probably had more recipes for "foolproof" fudge than anyone. While some laid a flower on her casket, one grandson produced a tiny Snickers bar which he left for her among the roses.

And we each have private memories that we take out and run through our fingers like jewels. They are harder to share. For me, Mimi was safe haven. It was always to Mimi's I headed with children too

whiny to go to the mall or hurt feelings that needed airing. Or even just to take a quick nap on the sofa while we watched a soap opera together. The last month, I laid down on the bed with her and we talked. Simple things. Where the kids were going. Her life. Her death. "How long do you think this will go on?" she asked. Those times were a gift. Others came and had their time, their gifts. Things that do not, even now, lend themselves to words. The terrible honor and pain of caring for someone you love with your own hands.

Her last day was magic, suspended somewhere just above reality; we all knew it would be the last. The day before Good Friday—Maundy Thursday. We washed her feet. Her Last Supper was a few drops of Pepsi dripped into her mouth with a straw. My children went to visit and were rewarded with a kiss and a beatific smile. Goodbye, goodbye, all the shadows whispered, our hearts pounded and our eyes spilled over. Goodbye. How can we say goodbye? But it was time, and we knew the hard business of dying had reached its end. So, like the third stage of labor in its clenched-teeth inescapable reality, dying was hard upon us. Mimi, passing.

The headstone is set now, and an urn for flowers. The raw gash of fresh dirt is weathering and runners of new St. Augustine grass reach across its middle. When I visit Mimi there I look around the cemetery. There is comfort, somehow, in the sheer numbers. So many people waiting patiently, all laid neatly facing east, waiting for the Lord. I smile and nod at old acquaintances as I pass their markers. There is even a headstone with my own name cut deeply into white stone; my passing, waiting on the horizon. My heart leaps at the hope that is stronger than sorrow. Goodbye, Mimi, goodbye.

ONE DEATH

Geraldine Connolly

When my grandmother was dying
in her soft bed in the corner
of my aunt's farmhouse kitchen,
we all sat with her, even the children

staring at the white, shut face,
masked in a rapture of its own
while all the noisy racket of death
filled the air, lungs letting go,

blood about to rise in a purple wash,
the pot of bones knocking,
in a fury to stay behind, stay with us.
Or perhaps the soul was rattling

its grip, a last hold on life,
giving the body one final slap,
she shuddered and trembled so, then
shook it all off and turned away.

I knew when the spirit left, her body
cold and floury, so still. We gave her
bed rail one last shove, helping
give her over to whatever pulled at her

from that other world. She no longer waited
as women wait but held forth one arm,
buoyant as that white branch the angel brought
both to warn and to comfort.

THE EMPRESS OF SCENTS
AND NON-SCENTS

Jan Henrikson

"A woman who wears no perfume has no future."   —*Paul Valery*

My parents barred me from the funeral so I had to take their word for it. Gramma Flo was dead.

Never again would she buy us a two-pound box of Fanny May's Nuts and Cremes and devour it all by herself. Nor would she smother me against her lily-of-the-valley-scented body and tell me tales about the man on her block found dead in his Buick, a rope coiled around his neck.

I was nine and hysterical. She was the first person I'd ever loved who'd died. She wasn't just a grandmother; she was a ritual. A blonde, fuzzy-faced, three-hundred-pound Empress, glittering in blue rhinestones. She ruled our universe.

Every Sunday morning we made a pilgrimage to her house in a section of Chicago where gangsters once massacred each other. Their descendants now displayed "Helping Hand" signs in their windows.

All day long, Gramma Flo majestically swelled into her green chair behind the card table in the living room, her enormous jiggling arms snapping a deck of cards or rattling dice as we three granddaughters gathered around her, ready to receive the seventy years of wisdom she finely distilled into one Gem of the Week.

"Girls! Girls! Always eat crusts! Remember that! Crusts make your hair curly!"

She lavished praise on my dad, her chosen son, the *good* son, and stared at my quiet and tired mother as if she were a very large eggplant.

We all knew our places in her kingdom, even if we didn't always like

them. Everything was set and safe in the fortress of her big arms, big lap, big love.

Now that she was dead, even laughter was dangerous. The song "Don't ever laugh when a hearse goes by for you may be the next to die," haunted me nightly. "The worms crawl in, the worms crawl out, the worms play peek-a-boo in your snout." The verses rang through my head. The image was horrifying, especially since we looked alike.

Suddenly that summer, the summer humankind landed on the moon, Gramma Flo landed in our house. Although we couldn't see her, the scent was unmistakable.

Lily of the valley enveloped our basement, hovered over the ping pong table and evaporated, returning the next week in the kitchen.

We desperately sniffed every random object just to make sure it wasn't some subtle, lingering fragrance of our own.

One morning the "Gramma Smell," as it came to be known, permeated the garage. That afternoon we received a phone call saying her house had finally been sold.

Dad was elated. Confirmation, at last! The mother he feared he'd lost forever was showering us with her celestial essence. Mom was stunned and speechless at the prospect of spending an infinity under Gramma Flo's rule.

I was strangely petrified. This didn't feel right. Other grandmothers died and soared to heaven. Why did mine float forty miles north to the suburbs?

"She's just letting us know she's all right," Dad winked. "She's looking out for us."

I refused to sleep. We never knew when or where she'd waft or who would smell her next. Every time I closed my eyes, I felt the bed spinning down into the dark and dungeoned basement where mutant forms of Gramma Flo lurked behind boxes and toys and cement poles.

I kept reliving a story I had once read about a little boy sick and dying in intensive care. One night the boy weakly lifted his right hand from the bed. Jesus appeared in a flash and instantly pulled his soul from his body, like a rabbit out of a hat. I slept on my hands for weeks after that,

fearful of sending Jesus the fatal signal.

Now Gramma Flo was the omniscient spirit waiting and watching my every move. I lay frozen in bed, swallowing my breath hard, staring at the bedroom window. I terrified my little sister into staring at the bedroom door just in case Gramma or some bogeywoman posing as Gramma decided to materialize.

Questions breathed menacingly from the shadows of my room: Why didn't this chatterbox speak? Why these perfume performances? Where was Grampa, who'd died ten years earlier? Was Gramma lonely? Did she want us to join her?

I wanted some answers and I wanted them fast. I turned to my best friend Katie who seemed like an expert on these things. "A seance," she whispered solemnly. "We must have a seance."

During lunch that week, we sneaked into a dark empty music practice room at our grade school. Katie began plucking wild, off-key notes from her bass violin. I closed my eyes and anxiously picked the fiddle that had once belonged to Grampa. "Come back, Gramma Flo." I started to chant. "Gramma Flo, Gramma Flo, come back, come back, come back."

Suddenly the door thundered open. White light seared the air. "What in the world are you doing?" boomed our music instructor. Katie and I screamed, then dissolved into a heap of nervous giggles.

I wanted to perform the seance again as soon as possible. "You're nuts," Katie crossed her eyes. "So's your dad. No one ever comes back. They go to heaven and sit on a long row of chairs in a cloud. Forever. There's a chair waiting for you."

At that moment, all the atoms within my nine-year-old body began zinging and snapping with the glad tidings of the truth she spoke. I was miraculously electrified with the Wisdom of the Ages.

Dad was merely a wistful, eccentric son missing his mom. Gramma Flo was sitting somewhere, unscented, in her green lumpy chair far above us all.

For a few seconds, I was safe.

More than twenty years later, I am as open to the secrets of the wind as Dad. As adventurous as the grandmother who travels from unknown places to fill our lives with fragrance. I choose crazy over safe. Today whenever lily of the valley swirls around me, I throw back my head, shake my generous nose, and dance in it.

SECOND LANGUAGE

(for Anastasia Chwastyc)

Andrena Zawinski

"No one ever told us we had to study our lives, making of
our lives a study, as if learning about natural history."
Adrienne Rich, "Transcendental Etude"

In that long moment before sleep sets in,
when the clock ticks above the silence,
I think of her. She was the woman who named
the world for me in patchwork Russian. Baba,
studa baba, rolled her socks down to the ankles,
wrapped silver braids beneath babushkas,
thought dressing up was wearing a fresh apron.
Baba trained my fingers to press pirogi dough,
never scolded when I ate the filling first;
tied my hair in rags, shaped long ringlets
round my full moon old world face.

Her bony fingers and milky eyes composed
a code of gesture and glance, as years grew
too large for speech beneath the handed down
command: *speak English.* She continued
the rituals of the years—kneading Sunday
paska, waxing *pysanka mandalas* to Easter eggs,
spreading thirteen Christmas foods for feast
across one prized lace tablecloth survivor
of Ellis Island and careless children.

It is in the quiet chill of this wintry night
that the thought of her keeps me up, that I know
these things, repeat her poultice cures, sing her
gypsy tales, recant a cruse, envision death.
This storms my dream: they say her deathbed gaze
was on my face, that she died of natural causes,
silence and superstition. And I am left now
to trace her name in wide black crosses, follow
her journey through challenged borders
of her Carpathian wilderness, left to salvage
my inheritance.

LITTLE ALBA

from *The House of the Spirits*

Isabel Allende

Alba was born feet first, which is a sign of good luck. Her Grandmother Clara searched her back and found the tiny star-shaped mark that distinguishes those born to true happiness. "There's no need to worry about this little girl. She will be lucky and she will be happy. She will also have a good complexion, because that is inherited, and at my age I have no wrinkles and I've never had a pimple," Clara declared two days after the birth. This is why they made no effort to prepare the child for life, since the stars had already conspired to endow her with so many gifts. Her sign was Leo. Her grandmother studied her astrological chart and recorded her destiny in white ink in an album with pages of black paper, in which she also pasted the child's first greenish locks of hair, the fingernails she clipped soon after her birth, and various portraits that allow one to see her as she was then: an extraordinarily tiny creature, almost bald, creased and pale, with no other sign of human intelligence than her sparkling black eyes, which bore an expression of ancient wisdom even when she was in the cradle. They were identical to those of her real father. Her mother wanted to call her Clara, but her grandmother didn't believe in repeating names, because it created confusion in her notebooks that bore witness to life. They searched for a name in a thesaurus, where they found hers, the last in the chain of luminous words. Years later, Alba tormented herself with the thought that when she had a daughter there would be no other word with the same meaning to use as a name, but [Alba's mother] Blanca gave her the idea of using other languages, which offer a wide choice. . . .

Age and experience had sharpened Clara's ability to divine the occult and to move objects from afar. An exalted state of mind could easily put her into a trance in which she would move around the room

while sitting in a chair, as if there were a hidden motor underneath the cushions. It was also during that time that a starving young artist, who had been given lodging in the house out of pity, paid for his stay by painting the only extant portrait of Clara. Much later, the impoverished artist was recognized as a master and today the painting hangs in a London museum, like so many works of art that left the country when people had to sell their furnishings to feed the victims of persecution. The canvas shows a middle-aged woman dressed in white, with silvery hair and the sweet gaze of a trapeze artist, resting in a rocking chair that hangs suspended just above the floor, floating amidst flowered curtains, a vase flying upside down, and a fat black cat that observes the scene like an important gentleman. Influence of Chagall, according to the catalogue, but that is not true. The picture captures precisely the reality the painter witnessed in Clara's house. That was the period when the divine good humor of the hidden forces of human nature acted with impunity to provoke a state of emergency and upheaval in the laws of physics and logic. Clara's communication with wandering souls and extraterrestrials was conducted through telepathy, dreams, and the pendulum she used for that purpose, dangling it in the air above an alphabet she had arranged in proper order on the table. The pendulum's autonomous movement pointed to the letters forming messages in Spanish and Esperanto, which proved that these, and not English, were the only languages of interest to beings from other dimensions, as Clara wrote in letters to the ambassadors of the English-speaking powers. They never answered her, and neither did the various ministers of education whom she wrote in order to explain her theory that instead of teaching English and French, which were languages for sailors, peddlers, and money lenders, the schools should insist that all the children in the country study Esperanto.

Alba's childhood was a mixture of vegetarian diets, Japanese martial arts, Tibetan dance, yogic breathing, relaxation and concentration with Professor Hausser, and many other interesting techniques, not to mention the contribution to her education made by her two uncles and the three enchanting Mora sisters. Her Grandmother Clara managed to

keep that immense covered wagon of a house rolling with its population of eccentrics, even though she had no domestic talent and disdained the basic operations of arithmetic to the point of forgetting how to add. The daily organization of the household and the keeping of accounts therefore fell to Blanca, who divided her time between the job of chief steward of that miniature kingdom and her work at her ceramic studio in the back of the courtyard, the ultimate refuge for her sorrows, where she gave classes for both mongoloids and young ladies and created incredible creches full of monsters which, against all logic, sold like hotcakes. . . .

Alba did not go to school; her grandmother held that anyone as favored by the stars as she was needed only to know how to read and write, and she could learn that at home. Clara was in such a hurry to make her literate that at the age of five the little girl was already reading the newspaper over breakfast and discussing the news with her grandfather. At six she discovered the magic books in the enchanted trunks of her legendary Great-Uncle Marcos and had fully entered the world-without-return of the imagination. Nor did anyone worry about her health; they did not believe in the benefits of vitamins and thought that vaccinations were for chickens; besides her grandmother studied the lines of her hand and said that she was made of iron and was assured of a long life. The only frivolous attention they lavished on her was to comb her hair with bay rum to mitigate the dark-green hue it had when she was born. . . . Alba gave up the bay rum as an adolescent and rinsed her hair with parsley water, which allowed the green to reappear in its full leafiness. The rest of her was tiny and innocuous as opposed to the other women in her family, who were, almost without exception, splendid.

One Christmas eve, Clara gave her granddaughter a fabulous present . . . a box filled with jars of paint, brushes, a small ladder, and permission to use the biggest wall in her bedroom whenever she wanted.

"This will give her an outlet for her feelings," Clara said, watching Alba, balanced on the ladder, painting a train full of animals just below the ceiling.

With the passage of time, Alba filled not only one but all her bedroom walls with an immense fresco. In the midst of Venusian flora

and an impossible fauna of invented animals much like those Rose had embroidered on her tablecloth and Blanca baked in her kiln, she painted all the wishes, memories, sorrows, and joys of her childhood. . . .

One day an old friend of Clara's came to [her] house with her grandson, a fat, soft teenager with the round face of a docile moon and an expression of unchanging tenderness in his tiny Oriental eyes. He was fifteen, but Alba realized he was like a baby. Clara asked her granddaughter to take the boy out to play in the garden and make sure he did not soil his clothes, drown in the fountain, eat dirt, or play with his fly. Alba quickly tired of watching him, and when she saw it was impossible to communicate with him in any coherent language, she took him to the ceramic studio, where Blanca, to keep him amused, tied an apron around him to protect him from stains and water and placed a ball of clay in his hands. The boy played with it for more than three hours, shaping a number of crude figures that he took to show his grand-mother. This lady, who had practically forgotten he was with her, was utterly delighted; thus the idea was born that ceramics was good for mongoloids. Blanca ended up giving classes to a group of children who came to her studio every Thursday afternoon. They were delivered by truck and escorted by two nuns in starched white coifs, who sat in the garden drinking chocolate with Clara and discussing the virtues of cross-stitching and the hierarchy of sin, while Blanca and her daughter taught the children how to fashion worms, balls, squashed dogs, and misshapen vases. At the end of the year the nuns organized an exhibition and a party, and the dreadful works of art were sold for charity. Blanca and Alba had quickly understood that the children worked much better when they felt loved, and that the only way to communicate with them was through affection. They learned to hug them, kiss them, and fondle them until they wound up genuinely loving them. Alba waited all week for the truck with the retarded children to come, and she jumped with glee when they ran to hug her. But those Thursdays wore them out. Alba fell asleep exhausted, the sweet Asiatic faces of the children spinning in her mind, and Blanca invariably had a migraine. After the nuns left, their herd of mongoloids in hand and their white wings aflutter, Blanca hugged her daughter passionately, covered her face with kisses, and told her they could thank God that she was normal. For this reason, Alba grew up thinking that normality was a gift from heaven. She discussed this with her grandmother.

"In almost every family there's a fool or a crazy person," Clara assured her while she concentrated on her knitting—in all those years she had not learned to knit without looking. "You can't always see them; they are kept out of sight as if they were something to be ashamed of. They are locked up in the back room so visitors won't see them. But actually there is nothing to be ashamed of. They're God's creatures too."

"But there's no one like that in our family, Grandmother," Alba replied.

"No. Here the madness was divided up equally, and there was nothing left over for us to have our own lunatic."

This was how their conversations with Clara went, and why, for Alba, the most important person in the house and the strongest presence in her life was her grandmother. She was the motor that drove the magic universe that was the rear section of the big house on the corner, where Alba spent her first seven years in complete freedom. She grew accustomed to her grandmother's eccentricities. She was not surprised, for example, to see her moving around the room in a trance, seated in an armchair with her arm tucked under her, pulled by an invisible force. She followed her on pilgrimages to hospitals and almshouses, where Clara tried to track down her needy flock; she even learned, using four-ply wool and enormous needles, to knit the sweaters her Uncle Jaime gave away after he had worn them once, just so she could see her grandmother's toothless smile while she squinted at the stitches. The little girl also took part in the Friday sessions, during which the three-legged table jumped in broad daylight without the aid of any special tricks, known form of energy, or outside leverage, as well as the literary soirees where she mingled with the acclaimed masters and a varying group of timid unknown artists whom Clara encouraged.

Clara was still young, but to her granddaughter she looked very old because of her missing teeth. She had no wrinkles, and when her mouth

was closed she gave the impression of extreme youth because of the innocent look on her face. She wore tunics of raw linen that looked like the robes crazy people wear, and in the winter she wore long woolen socks and fingerless gloves. She laughed at things that were not the least bit funny; on the other hand, she was incapable of understanding any joke, always laughing at the wrong time, and she could become very sad if she saw someone else behaving in a ridiculous fashion. Sometimes she had asthma attacks and would summon her granddaughter with a tiny silver bell she always carried on her person. Alba would come running to embrace her with consoling whispers, since they both knew from long experience that the only cure for asthma is the prolonged embrace of a loved one. She had laughing hazel eyes, shiny hair flecked with white and pulled into an untidy bun from which rebellious wisps escaped, and fine white hands with almond-shaped nails and long ringless fingers, which were useless except when it came to gestures of affection, arranging her divining cards, or putting in her denture before meals. Alba spent the day trailing after her, snuggling into her skirts and begging her to tell one of her stories or move the vases with the power in her mind. She found in her grandmother a sure refuge when she was haunted by nightmares. . . . Clara taught her how to take care of birds and speak to each of them in its own language, as well as how to read the premonitions in nature and knit chain-stitch scarves for the poor.

Alba knew that her grandmother was the soul of the big house on the corner. Everybody else learned it later, when Clara died and the house lost its flowers, its nomadic friends, and its playful spirits and entered into an era of decline.

Clara died on Alba's seventh birthday. The first omen of her death was perceptible only to her. She began to make secret preparations to depart. With great discretion she divided up her clothing among the servants and the followers she always had, keeping only what she absolutely needed. She put her papers in order, and salvaged her notebooks that bore witness to life from the hidden corners of the house. She tied them up with colored ribbons, arranging them according to events and not in chronological order, for the one thing she had forgot-

ten to record was the dates, and in her final haste she decided that she could not waste time looking them up. When she was searching for the notebooks, the jewels began to appear in shoe boxes, in stocking wrappers, and on the bottom shelves of wardrobes, where she kept them ever since the days when her husband gave them to her hoping to win her love. She placed them in an old woolen sock, fastened it with a safety pin, and handed them to Blanca.

"Put this away, darling. Someday they may be good for something besides masquerades," she said.

Blanca discussed the matter with Jaime and he began to keep an eye on his mother. He noticed that she was leading an apparently normal life but that she barely ate, sustaining herself with milk and a few spoonfuls of honey. Nor did she sleep very much. She spent the night writing or wandering through the house. She seemed to be detaching herself from the world, growing ever lighter, more transparent, more winged.

"One of these days she's going to fly away," Jaime said, worried.

Suddenly, she began to suffocate. She felt the gallop of a wild horse in her chest and the anxiety of a rider rushing headlong into the wind. She said it was her asthma, but Alba noticed that she no longer rang the little silver bell so she would come and cure her with prolonged hugs. One morning she saw her grandmother opening the bird cages with inexplicable joy.

Clara wrote small cards to each of her loved ones, of whom there were many, and secretly placed them in a box beneath her bed. The next morning she did not get up, and when the maid brought in the breakfast tray she refused to have her open the curtains. She had begun to take leave even of the light, to enter slowly into darkness.

When he heard about this, Jaime went to see her. He insisted on examining her. He found nothing abnormal in her appearance, but he knew beyond a shadow of a doubt that she was going to die. He left her room with a broad, hypocritical smile, and once he was out of his mother's field of vision he had to lean against the wall, because his legs were giving out. He called a specialist from the school of medicine, who appeared that very day in the Trueba home. After seeing Clara, he

confirmed Jaime's diagnosis. They assembled the whole family in the drawing room and without much ado announced that she would not live more than two or three weeks and that the only thing to be done was to sit with her, so that she would die happy.

"I think she's decided to die, and science has no cure for that," said Jaime.

Estaban Trueba grabbed his son by the collar and was on the verge of choking him. He pushed the specialist out the door and smashed all the lamps and china in the room. Finally he fell to his knees, moaning like a newborn baby. Just at that moment, Alba entered the room and saw her grandfather reduced to her own height. She went up to him and stared him in the eyes, and when she saw his tears she threw her arms around him. It was the old man's weeping that told her what the matter was. She was the only one in the family who did not lose her serenity, thanks to her training in surmounting pain and the fact that her grandmother had often explained to her the circumstances and rituals of death.

"Just as when we come into the world, when we die we are afraid of the unknown. But the fear is something from within us that has nothing to do with reality. Dying is like being born; just a change," Clara had said.

She added that if she could easily communicate with those from the Hereafter, she was absolutely convinced that afterward she would be able to do the same with those of the Here-and-Now. Thus, instead of whimpering when the time came, she hoped Alba would be calm, because in her case death would not be a separation, but a way of being more united. Alba understood perfectly.

Soon afterward Clara seemed to enter a gentle sleep. Only the visible effort to take air into her lungs showed that she was alive. Still, asphyxiation did not seem to cause her undue anxiety now that she was not fighting for her life. Her granddaughter remained at her side the entire time. They had to improvise a bed for Alba on the floor because she refused to leave the room, and when they tried to take her out she had her first tantrum. She insisted that her grandmother was aware of everything and that she needed her. And this was true. Shortly before

the end, Clara regained consciousness and was able to speak calmly. The first thing she noticed was Alba's hand in hers.

"I'm going to die, aren't I, darling?" she asked.

"Yes, Grandmother, but it doesn't matter, because I'm here with you," the child replied.

"That's good. Take out the box of cards that's under the bed and hand them out, because I won't have time to say goodbye to everyone."

Clara closed her eyes, breathed a contented sigh, and left for the other world without looking back. . . .

HANGING THE WASH AT MIDNIGHT

Rebecca Baggett

Stars glow crisp, through a chill
that heralds frost. I bend
and straighten, clip damp cloth
to the line, not sure what
I'm hanging. Morning will find
shirts inside-out, socks unmated,
everything a little drunken,
a little bit awry.

I know exactly what Grandma would
think of this. I know how she
hung her washing, Monday mornings
early, every piece just so, grouped
by purpose, color, size, down the
long line stretched from house to
barn. Her creed: Have it out before
the neighbors. And have the neatest line.

Four weeks past her death,
the furniture's divided, clothing
and canned goods sorted, dust
of twenty years swept from corners
behind things, where she couldn't
reach. The rest was spotless,
purses and shoes aligned and gleaming
dimly from closet shelves, her
stockings rolled in soft, tight balls,
like small animals sleeping winter

through inside her drawers.
She'd have a fit if she could see
me. *Look at the girl*, she crabs
inside my head. *No wonder she can't
keep a proper house. Look how
she hangs those things up any way,
as if it didn't matter.*

"I expect," she sniffed once,
"that poets don't have dust cloths."
I've never been quite certain that
she liked me—or liked the woman
I became outside her door, who wrote
about people even before they'd died.
"In my day," she said, "we kept our
troubles to ourselves. And weren't
the worse for it." And, yes, that's
why I'm out here now—I spent the day
inside, cajoling words, while sheets
and towels soured in their baskets,
and the sun spilled all its light
on grass and trees.

I flex numbed fingers, staring at
the sky. She'd have a fit. Or link
her hand with mine, the way she did
the week before she died, bones
too near the surface, grating,
and her eyes entreating me to do
this work I claim as mine: to find
the words to get her out of this
or make some sense of it, transmute

this end to something bearable,
well-ordered at the least, the kind
of thing she might have planned
herself, while hanging wash one day,
something not entirely out of line.

BONE
OF MY BONES

"Families will not be broken.
Curse and expel them, send their children wandering,
drown them in floods and fires,
and old women will make songs out of all these sorrows
and sit on the porches
and sing them on mild evenings."
Marilynne Robinson

A GRANDMOTHER WORKBOOK

In talking to women about this anthology, the response was overwhelmingly enthusiastic. Some women had written pieces about grandmothers to submit. Others wanted to write something. Still others had thought about writing about their own grandmothers for years, but had never found the time to do so. And others, while they felt enthusiastic, were frightened by the idea of capturing her indelibly on paper. Since "Grandmother" conjures so much feeling, I invite you to write about her. This is an excellent way to grieve or to prepare yourself for her passing.

You may want to use this section as an exercise in remembering or use it for developing your creative expression. Or, you may want to use it to honor your grandmother. Whatever you do, if you do any of it, you will probably be changed. Writing can heal, soothe, excite, frustrate, and consummate. Simply put, writing is good therapy.

Clearly, this is not meant as an English writing class. Feel free to write without punctuation or capitalizations. Reserve the Internal Critic for final drafts of only those things you would want to share with others. Let the images flow onto the pages, then go back later and edit if you want. Play with sounds and rhythm, and stanza or line length when writing poetry. Forget previously ingrained notions about what is good or bad writing. *You* get to decide what you will share or not share. No one cares what you say or don't say. Say it all. Say it angrily, joyfully, hopefully, despairingly, or plainly. Draw a broad picture or focus on a small aspect, like a closeup in a photograph. Cry as you write. Laugh. Tear up a page and then write it all again differently. Let yourself go. This is between you and your grandmother.

After each selection you will find a topic question for writing about your grandmother. Let your imagination flow. If a question doesn't apply to your grandmother, write about a fantasy grandmother—something you might remember about her if she were real. Don't hurry. Take the time to really feel, think, and contemplate each of the topics. For certain topics, you may want to write several pieces that address the question. After some time of letting a piece sit, you may want to go back and add to it or write it from a different angle or outcome. Be persistent. You may think you have nothing to say about a certain aspect of these topic questions, but after some thought, you may find a wealth of memories or feelings.

Always try the option of writing about the opposite topic. For example, if the question asks you to write about something your grandmother did well, write about what she did poorly. If the instruction is to write about how she saw or treated you as special, write about how she didn't.

Keep your writings in a journal or three-ring binder. You may want to divide your writing into different sections, topics, or chapters which surface naturally. Give your book a title. Feel free to share this with your grandmother or family members. Feel free to keep it very private.

TOPIC QUESTIONS

Below is a list of topic questions for your writings. If you need help or get stuck, refer to the corresponding selection. Reread the selection, then let your own imagination consider the topic in relation to your grandmother.

1. Write a poem about something you did regularly with your grandmother. Write free verse. Don't concern yourself with grammar, rhyme, or stanza length. Play with these parameters.
   Masih
2. Write about a significant event that happened to your grandmother. Write prose or poetry. If you don't know the details, make them up.
   Angelou
3. Write about an ailment or affliction she had. Then add or write another piece about her unfailing spirit and how she overcame it.
   Atwood, Fisher, Maki
4. Write about how your grandmother was seen in the family. Include something that happened to her as a way of illustrating this. Write about

how it was or was not resolved. How was she seen by outsiders? What was her relationship like with them?

Ito, Silko

5. Write about a room or place in or around your grandmother's house that was significant to you as a child. Write about how you played in those places.

Rendrick

6. Write about how your grandmother frightened or embarrassed you. Consider what was behind this. What did you learn from it? Look for the good intention.

Roxas

7. Write about something your grandmother did that you found amazing, frightening, or awful. Let it show the difference in how the generations viewed sentimentality and pragmatism.

Moss, Shebar

8. Write about how your grandmother cared for her home. Choose a specific subject such as canning food, ironing sheets, or pulling weeds. Look for the relationship between these activities and her beliefs, values, or upbringing.

Atwood

9. What was bedtime like with her?

10. Write a funny story about something you and your grandmother did or about how she "got you."

Maki

11. What was her relationship with food? How did she tie you to her through her food? Describe cooking together. Describe a meal with her.

D'Angelo, Fisher, Hughes

12. Write about a talent or characteristic of your grandmother that made her "bigger than life."

Barrymore, Cooper, Kack-Brice

13. What do you remember about how your grandmother smelled, looked, or occupied space in a room?

Henrikson

14. How was life with grandmother slower, more connected to nature?

Nelms, Freeman-Toole

15. Did she scold you? How? What happened? Did she then make up for it somehow?

Atwood

16. Write about her life. Focus on a particular quality, lifestyle, orientation, habit, or choice she made. Good or bad. How was she an inspiration for you? Focus on a cultural or racial history.

Loren, Makofsky, Williams, Seale, Shebar

17. Write about her name. Is there a connection to your name? How did she speak your name?

Morris

18. What were her peculiar speech patterns or colloquialisms? How did you feel about this as a child? Did she speak another language?

Danforth, Hogan, Zawinski

19. What was your grandmother's own special brand of advice? Write a vignette or poem about these special words.

Caldwell, Markova

20. What did your grandmother feel strongly about? What were her political, moral, or spiritual views and how were you influenced by these? Write about them with humor.

Angelou, Patterson

21. What were the miracles that happened to your grandmother? What miracle did you share with her?

Allende, Vigil

22. Write about your membership in the lineage of women in your family. What is your relationship to these women? What have they given you?

Haiden, Hogan

23. What lessons or gifts do you continue to receive from the other side of her death? Do you dream of her? Do you feel her? Do you see her hands in yours as you work?

Markova, Moss, Freeman-Toole

24. Write about a box, purse, drawer, or the like, that contained your grandmother's things. What was the meaning of this to you? What did you learn about her from the contents therein?

Markova, Masih, Moss, Parlante

25. How was your grandmother's life an example of "appreciating the simple things?" Illustrate how the pace of her life was different from yours.

Freeman-Toole, Markova

26. In a very brief poem, perhaps a haiku, what were the most profound gifts you received from your grandmother?

27. Write about your grandmother's death. How did you participate in this? What was its meaning to you? What do you wish? How would you make it different? Prose or poem.

Baggett, Crooker, Connolly, Henrikson

28. Write a letter to your grandmother. Tell her what you never said. Tell her what you remember. Tell her what she didn't give you. Tell her what you wish for her, for you, for her great- grandchildren.

29. What do you think was her last wish? Did she get it or not? What do you feel about this?

Rich

30. Write about her hands, eyes, face, feet, breasts, bottom, nose.

Kack-Brice, Markova

31. Write about what you didn't like about her.

Patterson

32. How was she different from your idea of "grandmother"?

Allende, Roxas

33. Write about the relationship you didn't have with her.

Freeman-Toole

34. Write about her marriage or child-rearing practices and how you would do it (or have done it) differently.

35. How were you special (or not) to her?

Egbert

36. Interview family members and compile their remembrances about her into a book along with your writing. Make copies for your family if you feel comfortable doing so.

NOTES ON CONTRIBUTORS

Isabel Allende worked as a journalist for many years and began writing fiction in 1981 with *The House of the Spirits* and, later, *Of Love and Shadows* and *Eva Luna*. She left Chile after the coup in 1973, lived many years in Caracas, and now resides near San Francisco.

Maya Angelou is a poet, actress, screenwriter, director, singer, and writer of five volumes of her autobiography, *I Know Why the Caged Bird Sings*. She teaches at Wake Forest University in Winston-Salem, North Carolina.

Margaret Atwood is a Canadian writer who has authored more than thirty books, including novels, poetry, and literary criticism, which have been translated into twenty languages and published in over twenty five countries. She lives in Toronto with her husband and daughter.

Rebecca Baggett lives in Athens, Georgia. Her poems, short stories, and essays have appeared in numerous publications.

Ethel Barrymore is considered one of America's greatest actresses. Devoted to acting despite a love for the concert piano, she appeared on stage with various family members from the age of fifteen, then made films, and was eventually awarded an honorary doctorate from New York University in 1952.

Beth Brant is a Mohawk of the Turtle Clan who lives in Detroit, where she was born. In addition to her many articles and poems in magazines and anthologies of Native American literature, she established an archive and library of information about Native American women called Turtle Grandmother.

E. K. Caldwell is a mixed-blood (Tsalgi, Creek, Shawnee, Celtic, and German) poet-writer whose poetry and short stories have been anthologized in the United States and Canada. She writes regularly for *Inkfish* magazine and *News from Indian Country* and is a member of the Native Writers Circle of the Americas.

Geraldine Connolly holds an M.A. in English from the University of Maryland. She has received fellowships and prizes for her poetry, has published two chapbooks, and teaches at the Writers Center in Bethesda, Maryland, where she lives with her husband and two children.

Amy Cooper, like her grandmother, spends a lot of time reading, writing, and cooking at her home in Batavia, Illinois. She holds a B.A. in English and art from Elmhurst College and hopes to write a longer story about her grandmother illustrated with her own drawings.

Barbara Crooker has published her award-winning poetry in numerous magazines, anthologies, and books. Her grandmother, Annunicata (Emma) Cuccaro Poti, emigrated from Picerno, Italy, when she was thirteen and lived to be ninety-one.

Mary D'Angelo has had poetry, fiction, and essays appear in more than a hundred publications across the country. Her poetry collection is titled *The Boneyard,* and she has just completed her first novel.

Pauline Brunette Danforth is a White Earth Ojibwe Indian living in Minneapolis, where she is a college adviser, tends her garden, and shares a love of history with her husband. She is attaining her Ph.D. in American studies at the University of Minnesota.

Gay Davidson-Zielske is a poet and fiction writer whose work has most recently appeared in *Eleven Wisconsin Poets.* She currently teaches composition, creative writing, and screenwriting at the University of Wisconsin–Whitewater and lives in Madison with her husband and son.

Toi Derricotte is a poet and teacher of poetry who was born in Detroit and now lives in New Jersey. Her work has appeared in many journals and anthologies, as well as her own publications, *The Empress of the Death House* and *Natural Birth.*

Kathlyn Whitsitt Egbert is the author of the highly praised novel *The 23rd Dream.* She lives in the Mexican border region of South Texas with her husband and their two daughters.

Carolyn J. Fairweather Hughes lives with her husband and two daughters in Pittsburgh, Pennsylvania. Her poetry has appeared in many anthologies and journals.

M. F. K. Fisher was raised in Whittier, California, and lived her last twenty years until 1992 in a house in a Napa vineyard. She published sixteen books, novels, and an autobiography, many on the subject of food and her early years in France.

Louise Freeman-Toole holds a B.A. in creative writing and lives with her husband and two sons in Pullman, Washington. Her poetry, nonfiction, and photography have appeared in newspapers and magazines around the country.

Mary Freericks conducts poetry residencies for California Poet in the Schools. She has an M.F.A. in poetry from Columbia University School of Arts writing division and a fellowship from the New Jersey State Council on the Arts. Her work has appeared in numerous publications.

Gangaji, formerly Antoinette Roberson Varner, travels around the world holding *satsang* for spiritual seekers. She was given the name Gangaji by her teacher Sri H.W.L. Poonja who requested that she speak to others of her spiritual realization.

Christina Gombar lives in New York City and has just received her master's degree in creative writing at City University. She received the Geraldine Griffin Moore Award for her novella, *The Heartbreaker*, and the Goodman Fund Loan Grant for a book she is writing on American women writers.

Jewelle Gomez is the author of a novel, *The Gilda Stories*, and a collection of essays, *Forty-Three Septembers*. She is a freelance writer living in San Francisco, where she is writing a dramatic adaptation of her novel.

Jan Henrikson is a freelance writer and nanny living in Tampa, Florida, with her partner, Robert. She has been a granddaughter for thirty-three years and, like her grandmother, enjoys traveling.

Virginia Haiden is a Minneapolis writer of award-winning poetry which has appeared in a variety of journals and anthologies. She is a mother and grandmother, an avid rock hound, and she loves ethnic cooking, gardening, and jewelry design.

Linda Hogan was born in Denver, attended the University of Colorado at Boulder, and now lives in Minneapolis. She has published many books of poetry, including *Calling Myself Home* and *Eclipse*, and is involved in community development and wildlife rehabilitation.

Susan Ito lives in Oakland, California, with her husband and two daughters; her youngest, Emma Asano, is named for Obasan. Her fiction and poetry have appeared in many journals and anthologies, and she currently teaches Rice Papers, a writing workshop for Asian American women.

B. K. Loren currently teaches literature and writing at De Anza College near Menlo Park, California. Her fiction and nonfiction have been published in numerous journals. She would like to dedicate this essay to her grandmother, Pearl Hall Clark, and her mother, Marjorie Loren Koontz.

Marjorie Maki is a former reporter and retired district director of the U.S. Customs Service. She free-lances for the Little Suburban Press in St. Paul, Minnesota.

Serena Makofsky lives and works in Oakland, California, within an hour's drive to her Nana. She is currently writing a novel about a young woman's journey across America in search of purpose and identity.

Dawna Markova, PhD. is a senior research affiliate of the Organizational Learning Center at MIT and the author of *The Art of the Possible*, *How Your Child IS Smart* and *No Enemies Within*. She is passionately interested in the creative process, collective learning, and the internal aspects of social change.

Tara L. Masih received an M.A. in professional writing and publishing from Emerson College and since then has published award winning-fiction, poetry, and essays in various literary magazines and anthologies. For three years she was assistant editor for *Stories*, a national literary magazine, and now works as a freelance book editor and writer in Andover, Massachusetts.

Carolyn S. Mateer is a retired librarian and lifelong lover of books. She grew up in a small Pennsylvania village of 250 people and now lives in a large metropolitan area in Washington State, more than light years away from her grandmother's world and milieu.

Helen Michaelson teaches English and Spanish in New York City. She has produced a musical comedy and recently completed a novel, *Romeo v. Juliet.*

Dilys Morris lives in the woods of New Hampshire, where she writes, sews, paints, cuts firewood, hauls water, and spends time with friends and her mostly grown, wonderful daughters. She holds graduate degrees from Harvard in ethics and government.

Riki Moss is a visual artist living on an island in Lake Champlain. Born in Brooklyn, she attended the San Francisco Art Institute, earned her M.F.A. from Vermont College, and is coauthor of *It's a Lot Like Dancing.*

Sheryl L. Nelms holds a B.S. from South Dakota State University and has taught writing workshops in colleges and writers' conferences. Besides being a prolific writer, she is a photographer, weaver, painter, and an old dirt biker.

Sharon Olds has written award-winning poetry in *Satan Says, The Dead and the Living,* and *The Father.* She was educated at Stanford and Columbia Universities and now teaches poetry workshops in the graduate creative writing program at NYU and at Goldwater Hospital.

Joanna Pashdag is a writer living in Los Angeles, where her hobbies include dancing, horseback riding, and kissing frogs.

Shelley Parlante lives with her husband and teenaged daughter in Orinda, California. She has worked in various kinds of science writing and publishing, is an editor for the Benjamin/Cummings Publishing Company, and has a special love for writing poetry.

Stephanie Patterson is a clinical social worker with an MSW from Bryn Mawr College and a freelance writer in Philadelphia. She has written on social implications of physical disability for the local press, and her essay "Someone has to care about Kierkegaard" appears in *The Book Group Book.* She lives and writes in Philadelphia, Pennsylvania.

Marge Piercy is a poet and novelist born in Detroit, now living in Massachusetts. She has many publications including *Woman on the Edge of Time, Mars and Her Children,* (poetry) and *The Longings of Women,* and has received many awards and grants for her work.

Bernice Rendrick is a writer living in Scotts Valley, California. She is studying with the Writer's Union poetry group and has published her poetry in several journals and anthologies.

Susanna Rich is an associate professor of English at Kean College of New Jersey and author of *The Flexible Writer*. Her poem is part of a full-length manuscript on her grandmother entitled "Never Was a Wolf."

Savina Roxas holds an M.F.A. and a Ph.D. from the University of Pittsburgh. Her award-winning poetry and short stories have appeared in various literary magazines and anthologies, and her chapbook of poems, *Sacrificial Mix*, was published in 1992.

Mary Scott, a poet since the age of fourteen, lives in Ventura, California, with her husband, Don, and is raising three children. She is looking forward to being a grandmother herself, but not anytime soon.

Jan Epton Seale has three books of poems, *Bonds, Sharing the House,* and *Quartet,* and a short-story collection, *Airlift.* She has held an NEA fellowship, and seven of her stories have appeared in Syndicated Fiction Projects.

Aile Shebar is a midwife and nurse, traveler, and bread baker like her grandmother Rae, and a lover of words and a good story, like her mother. She resides part time in Santa Fe, New Mexico, near her daughter, and currently visits India and Southeast Asia each year to work and write.

Leslie Marmon Silko lives in Tucson and teaches at the Universities of Arizona and New Mexico. In addition to her many awards and grants, she has published poetry and prose: *Laguna Woman: Poems; Ceremony; Storyteller;* and *Almanac of the Dead.*

Kiran A. Thakare was born in India and raised in Mahatma Gandhi's Ashram in Sewagram. She is a computer engineer graduate from Ohio University and hopes to return to her native country. In the meantime, she lives in Athens, Ohio, and loves to ride horses.

Lisa Williams is a poet and writer living in New York City. Her work has appeared in various journals, and she is currently finishing a doctoral dissertation on Virginia Woolf at the CUNY Graduate Center.

Lilly Mary Vigil is the owner of a gallery and shop in Nevada City, California, which supports Native American artists.

Andrena Zawinski teaches in the Pittsburgh public schools and is a teacher consultant for the West Pennsylvania Writing Project at the University of Pittsburgh. Her book of poems, *Traveling in Reflected Light,* was awarded the Kenneth Patchen Prize for Poetry from Pig Iron Press.

PERMISSIONS ACKNOWLEDGMENTS

*Thanks to the authors and publishers who
gave permission to excerpt from the following works:*

Allende, Isabel: "Chapter Nine, Little Alba" from *The House of the Spirits* by Isabel Allende, copyright © 1985, Alfred A. Knopf, Inc. Reprinted by permission of Alfred A Knopf, Inc. Angelou, Maya: "Chapter 5" from *I Know Why the Caged Bird Sings* by Maya Angelou, copyright © 1969 by Maya Angelou. Reprinted by permission of Random House Inc. Atwood, Margaret: "Bodily Harm" from *Bodily Harm* by Margaret Atwood, copyright © 1983, O. W. Toad, Ltd. Reprinted by permission of Simon & Schuster. Bagget, Rebecca: "Hanging the Wash at Midnight" first appeared in *MS* magazine, May/June 1992. Barrymore, Ethel: excerpted from *Memories: An Autobiography* by Ethel Barrymore, copyright © 1955 by Ethel Barrymore. Copyright renewed 1993 by Samuel Colt. Reprinted by permission of HarperCollins Publishers, Inc. Brant, Beth: "Native Origin" from *Mohawk Trail* by Beth Brant, Firebrand Books, Ithaca, NY, copyright © 1985 by Beth Brant. Crooker, Barbara: "Recipe for Grief," West Branch, 1984, and *Anthology of Magazine Verse and Yearbook of American Poetry*, 1985; also in *The Lost Children* by Barbara Crooker, Heycheck Press, 1989. Davidson-Zielske, Gay: "Cottonbound," *Towers*, Northern Illinois University's student literary magazine, 1975, and Survival Graphics' 1994 Calendar. Derricotte, Toi: "The Weakness" from *Captivity* by Toi Derricotte, copyright © 1989 by Toi Derricotte. Reprinted by permission of the University of Pittsburgh Press. Fisher, M. F. K.: "Grandmother's Nervous Stomach (1913–1920)" from *To Begin Again* by M. F. K. Fisher, copyright © 1993 by M. F. K. Fisher Literary Trust. Reprinted by permission of Pantheon Books, a division of Random House Inc. Gomez, Jewelle: "I Lost It at the Movies" from *Forty-Three Septembers* by Jewelle Gomez, Firebrand Books, Ithaca, NY, copyright © 1993 by Jewelle Gomez. Reprinted by permission of the publisher. Scott, Mary: "Personal Effects" first appeared in *Amelia,* 1988. Hogan, Linda: "The Grandmother Songs" first appeared in *The Book of Medicines* by Linda Hogan, Coffee House Press, 1993, copyright © 1993 by Linda Hogan. Reprinted by permission of the publisher. Ito, Susan: "Obasan in Suburbia" first appeared in *Womanist* magazine, Spring 1993. Nelms, Sheryl L.: "heirloom hocked" has appeared in *Magical Blend* magazine, 1982, *Cottage Cheese* in July 1986, *Tapjoe* in March 1990, and *Strawberries & Rhubarb* in 1990. Olds, Sharon: "Birthday Poem for My Grandmother" reprinted from *The Dead and the Living*, 1983, Alfred A. Knopf Inc. Reprinted by permission of the publisher. Piercy, Marge: "For She Is a Tree of Life" from *Mars and Her Children* by Marge Piercy, copyright © 1992 by Middlemarsh Inc. Reprinted by permission of Alfred A. Knopf Inc. Rendrick, Bernice: "The trunk in the Attic," *Sonoma Mandala Literary Review*, 1988, Sonoma State University. Rich, Susanna: "The Buck" first appeared in *South Coast Poetry Journal* No. 13, June 1993. Seale, Jan